"Sam Moore is living proof that faith, freedom and family—with a healthy dose of hard work—are the crucial ingredients in the formula for success. Sam's inspiring story is a must read!"
Oliver North
Lt. Col. USMC (Ret.)

"The hand of a sovereign God reached into the heart of Lebanon and saved a child who would immigrate to America and shake the nations of the world as a publishing magnate. The autobiography of Sam Moore is must reading for every American. It is an epic of a man who reached the pinnacle of success against all odds."
Pastor John Hagee
Author of *Beginning of the End*

"Sam Moore's remarkable story reminds us that we are proud to be a nation of immigrants, but even prouder to say, 'We are all Americans.' "
Lamar Alexander
Founder of Campaign for a New American Century

"One of America's greatest national treasures writes the book that all Americans should read."
Dr. Robert H. Schuller
Founding Pastor, Crystal Cathedral Ministries and author

"Sam Moore's story is not just a book—it's an adventure. It's a cross cultural journey . . . an educational business model . . . a celebration of the American Dream. It's evidence that there is a God who still performs miracles. This is an inspiring story that will encourage and challenge you."
Peter Lowe
CEO, Peter Lowe International

"Sam Moore is the American dream personified. His heart for God and head for business are a model for anyone who desires success. His work has touched so many people's lives in a wonderfully positive way, including mine. I'm sure he will make an impact on you through the telling of his incredible story."
John C. Maxwell
Author, speaker, and founder of INJOY, Inc.

"This is a tremendous testimony to God as to how He works through brilliant men who lean on the Lord rather than depending on their own skills. Sam Moore yielded to God and God blessed his humility and faithfulness."
Bill McCartney
CEO Promise Keepers

"Only in America could the young Sam Moore arrive from his native Lebanon filled with Christian faith and ambition, confident that the land of freedom would offer him a chance to achieve his highest and best. Sam's life is an inspiration to all Americans, and to all who love freedom."
John Ashcroft
United States Senator, Missouri

"Sam Moore embraces America—the land of opportunity—and engages the reader to strive for excellence."
Dr. Beverly LaHaye
Chairman, Concerned Women for America

"Sam Moore has been a towering leader in the religious book publishing industry in America, a wonderful Christian and a true inspiration for all those who appreciate the opportunity that exists in America for those who have intelligence, initiative, and integrity to succeed."
Pat Robertson, Chairman
The Christian Broadcasting Network

"Amazing is only one word of many superlatives to describe Sam Moore. His intense drive for success is tempered by his compassion for those in need. His powerful business ability is mingled with a keen sense of humor. His Lebanese accent makes his love for America all the more challenging. This book will give insight into these and other qualities that make this man the unique individual that he is."
Adrian Rogers
Pastor, Bellevue Baptist Church
Memphis, Tennessee

"My friend, Sam Moore, is a shining example of an immigrant without money or friends who 'seized the opportunity' to put his spirit, mind, and hand to work . . . and has built a great publishing company for millions of people in many nations . . . remaining a humble man of integrity and vision whose life says to all of us, 'If Sam can do it—anybody can.' I admire Sam Moore as a Christian leader who is a 'shining light on a hill.' "
Oral Roberts

"The Sam Moore story is long overdue. What a powerful message of hope, perseverance, integrity, and faith."
Pat Williams
Senior Executive Vice President, Orlando Magic
Author of *Go For the Magic*

"This autobiography comes from the heart of a man who was sold on the Bible early in his life, and who in turn has sold more Bibles, than any man who ever lived, through his giant publishing firm of Thomas Nelson. From his youth in faraway Lebanon, he was a visionary who was also sold on America, and who incorporates in *American by Choice* his praise for the country that gave him a life of treasured freedom and phenomenal success as a Christian businessman. An inspiration to read!"
D. James Kennedy, Ph.D.
Author of *What If Jesus Had Never Been Born?*

"From his days as a young child in Lebanon to his life as a successful businessman in America, Sam reminds each of us what a privilege and honor it is to live in such a wonderful country. This book allows everyone to experience the remarkable jour-

ney that Sam has traveled and challenges us to achieve deeper meaning in all that we do."
Spencer Abraham
United States Senator

"Millions of lives have been affected for the better because of his vision and efforts. *American by Choice* gives encouragement to all of us by getting a glimpse of his journey."
Chris Christian

"Sam Moore's faith-based life is an inspiring and encouraging book to all pilgrims on their journey."
Holland H. Coors

"*American by Choice* is the exciting and inspiring reminder of what life in America can be when faith in God and determination are combined!"
Brock & Bodie Thoene
Bestselling Novelists

"Every business person should read *American by Choice*! It is fantastic! It will inspire you and teach you how to be successful—in business and in life."
Art Williams
President—A. L. Williams

"Sam Moore, through his faith in God and hard work, has succeeded where a lesser person would have given up. This is a most remarkable book by and about a most extraordinary man. Every person should read and study it."
Judge Paul Pressler
Texas Court of Appeals (Retired)

"The book is filled with Christian inspiration, intriguing philosophy and Sam's own formula for success."
David Stringfield
President & CEO, Baptist Hospital

"*American by Choice* captivates the reader because of the fascinating story of the fulfillment of an American dream. The fantastic perseverance and formidable faith in God's power to answer prayer generates in the reader an attitude of gratitude for people like Sam Moore."
Dr. Anis A. Shorrosh
Author, International Evangelist

"Sam Moore is a living example of how the American dream can be achieved and of how equality of opportunity is potentially available for all individuals in this country. His message should be a lesson of encouragement to all and especially to those who think that the odds for success are against them."
Dr. George Roche
President, Hillsdale College

"*American by Choice* provides a fascinating insight into the dynamics of success from a Christian perspective. This important book gives a warm and tender insight into Sam's early years and some important keys to success for anyone who reads it."
Dr. Theodore Baehr

"God's providence in Sam's life is an amazing record of what can be accomplished when an individual is yielded completely to Christ. *American by Choice,* will inspire, motivate, and encourage."
Jack Graham
Author of *Diamonds in the Dark*

"An inspiring love story. Every page of Sam Moore's memoir is suffused with love—love of his family, love of freedom, love of his adopted country, America, and love of the Bible he has done so much to bring to millions."
Edwin J. Feulner, Ph.D.
President, The Heritage Foundation

"Sam Moore is a great father, husband, entrepreneur, philanthropist, patriot and most of all, man of God. Sam is the personification of the American miracle. This book should be read by every young person who is dreaming of greatness, and every mature person who wants to be reminded of why America is so great."
Jerry Falwell
Chancellor, Liberty University

"Sam Moore is an American by Choice who has been chosen by God to further His Kingdom through the printed word. Anyone who puts his six principles of leadership into practice is certain to achieve greater success not only in business, but also in their personal lives."
Norm Miller
Chairman, Interstate Batteries
Author of *Beyond the Norm*

"Sam Moore demonstrates that the American Dream—with God's help—is alive and well. Every American should be required to read this story."
Paul M. Weyrich, President Free Congress Foundation

"*American by Choice* is not just another 'rags to riches' story. It is however, a riveting account of how an immigrant from Lebanon converts the American dream into a reality. Sam Moore's life story confirms that with faith in God all things are indeed possible. His personal and professional success serves as a blueprint to what can transpire when faith merges with hard work, perseverance, and fortitude."
Bishop Dwight D. Pate
Church Point Ministries
Baton Rouge, Louisiana

"Sam Moore rekindles a patriot pride in our American heritage and a deep thankfulness for the freedom and blessings we enjoy in this country. The history of Thomas Nelson is both remarkable and inspiring. Indeed, with God all things are possible."
Terry Meeuwsen
Co-host, "The 700 Club" and author

AMERICAN
BY
CHOICE

AMERICAN
BY
CHOICE

THE REMARKABLE FULFILLMENT OF AN IMMIGRANT'S DREAMS

BY SAM MOORE

THOMAS NELSON PUBLISHERS
Nashville

Published in Nashville, Tennessee, by Thomas Nelson, Inc.

An exhaustive search was done to determine whether any material published in this book required permission to print. If there has been an error, I apologize and a correction will be made in subsequent editions.

All profits from the sale of this book have been pledged to Christian mission efforts.

Scripture quotations noted NKJV are from the NEW KING JAMES VERSION. Copyright © 1979, 1980, 1982, Thomas Nelson, Inc., Publishers.

Scripture quotations noted KJV are from the King James Version of the Holy Bible.

Library of Congress Cataloging-in-Publication Data
Moore, Sam, 1930–
    American by choice : the remarkable fulfillment of an immigrant's dreams /
by Sam Moore.
        p.   cm.
    Includes bibliographical references (p.   ).
    ISBN 07852-7453-7
    1. Moore, Sam, 1930–   . 2. Publishers and publishing—United States—
Biography.   3. Lebanese Americans—Biography.   4. Thomas Nelson
Publishers—History.   5. Christian literature—Publication and distribution—
United States—History—20th century.   I. Title.
Z473.M84A3   1998
070.6′092—dc21
    [b]   97-48388
                                                                          CIP

Printed in the United States of America

1   2   3   4   5   6   7   BVG   04   03   02   01   00   99   98

Dedication

For my children Joseph Samuel, Sandra Lee, and Rachel Michelle. For the love of my life, my dear Peggy, my constant companion and closest friend. Thank you for being my wife.

Contents

Publishers Since 1798

"Unless the LORD builds the house,
They labor in vain who build it."
Psalm 127:1 NKJV

Acknowledgments

I want to thank my friend, the V. Rev. Fr. Peter Gillquist, for his considerable help in organizing all the material for this book and helping me to share the story of my life. Thank you Peter.

I want to thank my wife Peggy. She spent many hours helping me to remember so much of what has taken place over the years. She also read and carefully reviewed each draft as it was prepared. As always, she faithfully encouraged me at every turn. Thank you, Peggy. I love you.

To Rolf Zettersten, Curtis Lundgren and the team in editorial and marketing: thanks for your patient and helpful assistance.

To Brenda White and the production department: thanks for your help in typesetting and manufacturing this book on a very tight schedule.

Finally I want to thank my personal staff for their constant support throughout the entire time we worked on this book.

Prologue

The Big Board

It was the most prestigious day in the history of Thomas Nelson Publishers in the U.S., and certainly one of the most exciting days of my life.

Here we were, Joe Powers, our senior vice president and chief financial officer; our book executive, Byron Williamson; our music executive, Roland Lundy; my son, Joe Moore, who heads our gift division; and me. On this warm and sunny Monday morning, June 19, 1995, Thomas Nelson was being listed on the storied New York Stock Exchange—the NYSE.

I suppose one reason for my not-so-irrational exuberance was that not one in a thousand American companies can qualify for an invitation to be listed on the NYSE. It is an incredible privilege. For years, Thomas Nelson had been listed on the NASDAQ, which is generally comprised of companies starting out (although this is beginning to change), the so-called "small cap" companies. Being a part of the Big Board meant we would be listed on the exchange that has the greatest exposure for its companies in the worldwide markets.

It also occurred to me on this momentous morning that we were standing at the very place where historic captains of industry such as John D. Rockefeller, Henry Ford, and Tom Watson (the IBM mogul) had all stood when they listed their firms.

I was awestruck. A relatively small general and Christian publishing company would be listed among all these household-name corporations on the Big Board. The NYSE is, after all, the place where "the big money" is, where the trading activity is, and it's the place where the majority of stock investment worldwide takes place. In all honesty, when you are listed here you sense that, in some measure at least, you have arrived, that you are the best of the best.

But there was something else very significant that went through my mind that morning. This was such a great moment for me personally, one who had come from the small Middle Eastern country of Lebanon with barely $600 in my pocket more than forty years earlier. I had started out as a freshman at a small, unaccredited college in South Carolina, at first washing dishes and cleaning floors, and then selling books and Bibles door-to-door on endless hot summer days. I'll admit that I was crying that morning as I walked onto the floor of the New York Stock Exchange, an immigrant thanking God for His blessing and goodness to me over the years—something I know I have never deserved.

A Day in Manhattan

We had flown into New York out of Nashville the evening before on the seven o'clock flight. (It is a practice of mine, by the way, to not travel during the day. I think it's a waste of time and my time belongs to our stockholders. I always try to fly in the evening, after I have a good day's work under my belt, then have a bite to eat and get to bed before eleven. That way I can start out the next morning refreshed and caught up, having put in eight to ten hours of work the day before.)

We began the day with our friends at PaineWebber in Midtown, one of our primary investment bankers. After a quick cup of coffee, we hailed a cab and headed down to Wall Street and the New York Stock Exchange. Mr. Richard Grasso, the president of the NYSE, was on hand to greet us as we stepped onto the floor.

"Of all the companies on the NYSE," he told me, "Thomas Nelson represents values, it represents America, and it represents the very roots of our nation." How appropriate, too, that a first-generation Italian immigrant, another taproot to the American way of life, would be the president and chairman of the board of the NYSE.

Just before the market opening at 9:30 A.M., we were led up to the famous parapet where the bell is rung to begin and end the day. The vocal group Anointed, four young African-American Christian artists, sang the National Anthem with great gusto to the explosive applause of the traders on the floor below.

Then, just after the opening bell, I stepped forward and with great joy purchased the first one hundred shares of Thomas Nelson stock, under the symbol TNM—Thomas Nelson Media. I was so excited, I don't even remember the opening price!

Most people think of Thomas Nelson as a publisher, but over the years and especially in the last few, we have diversified into various media ventures. We have become much more than a "plain old publisher," so it seemed fitting and proper to choose a name that reflects our mission. We have corporate goals that will solidly position Thomas Nelson, Inc., as a steadily growing corporation in the coming years.

By now the trading day was well under way. I pondered the fact that if I had bought this same one hundred shares in the company twenty years earlier, I would have averaged 20 percent growth a year for those two decades. Or, to put it another way, a $1,000 purchase of Thomas Nelson stock in 1975, figuring in all of the stock splits and dividends, would have been worth $103,000 that day in 1995, more than a hundred-fold gain in twenty years. *Where else but in America?* I said to myself.

We completed our day by calling on a couple of customers in New York City, and then boarded the plane that evening to return to Nashville.

A Blessed Responsibility

The ancient prophets were right when they said, "Pride goes before destruction" (Prov. 16:18 NKJV). In recounting this and the various other successes this company has known in the pages that follow, I realize, at least in part, the tremendous weight of responsibility that is placed upon my shoulders. For the Scriptures also teach, "To whom much is given, from him much will be required" (Luke 12:48 NKJV).

The older I get, the more clearly I realize that even with the few years I have left in this world I am still basically a stranger and a pilgrim here. I brought nothing with me to this life and I will exit with even less! Rich or poor, apart from a personal knowledge of Christ and a love for Him and His kingdom, life here really is, in a word, empty.

So in telling the story of my life and the blessings that God has bestowed upon me, I will endeavor to do so with a spirit of thanksgiving and humility.

My goal is first and foremost to give glory to God.

Second, it is to show my gratitude as an immigrant for the great privileges and opportunities we enjoy as citizens of the United States of America. I am here by choice, not by birth.

Third, I will also try to give some brotherly advice to other businesspeople just starting out in their careers. I want to share lessons I have learned in my career that have brought some measure of success along the way. And I'll try to be candid. Any story has woven into its fabric both the things that were done right and the things that could have been done better. It's nothing new to remind ourselves that we learn by our mistakes.

I've always been, and remain today, a very driven, intense person. My greatest weakness is impatience—sometimes I can be patient, but I almost always have to work at it. Another weakness is a constant striving for perfection. It's not easy for me to accept that errors happen and life will go on anyway. Frankly, it's the little things that aggravate me more than the major catastrophes. I'm usually able to remain pretty calm and reserved when the big stuff goes haywire.

One of my assets, I suppose, is that God has enabled me to truly love people. I care about others and genuinely enjoy relating to other people. God has brought so many good men and women into my life that it would be impossible to tell about every single one of them. My wife, Peggy, is my greatest gift from God. Whether I mention all the others in these pages or not, I deeply appreciate the thousands of people who have been a part of my life as an American, as well as all of those with whom I grew up and knew in Lebanon before coming here. I thank God every day for my father and mother, all my brothers and sisters, and my grandparents. I love you all very much.

I still believe, with the poet Robert Browning, that "the best is yet to be." There's still more room for success in America. Certainly, the grace and mercy of God have been and always will be available to us, and especially to those who seek to follow Him with all their heart. For me, these two have gone hand in hand. In our business lives, in our family lives, and in our personal lives we are called to synergize, to work together with the Lord in everything that we do.

Because of His faithfulness, this is my story.

Foreword

Young Salim Ziady traded the war-riddled hills of Beirut for the hills of Tennessee. He came to America with $600 in his pocket, few acquaintances, and high aspirations. Within a few short years, he would change both his name (to Sam Moore) and the face of Christian publishing by purchasing Thomas Nelson Publishing.

But this is no typical "rags-to-riches" tale. For, though he may have had little change in his wallet when he left Lebanon, he was already rich in a more important commodity. Faith. Nineteen-year-old Salim was wealthy in the resource that never vanishes.

There were plenty of pitfalls and chug holes on the road that took Sam from door-to-door salesman to CEO of a company listed on the New York Stock Exchange. And through it all, Sam relied on an inextinguishable faith, giving him the confident trust that his God would guide him.

The story Sam has written is one I have been privileged to hear in person. May God use Sam's life to inspire yours. In a sense, we are all making a similar journey. Just like Sam, we are each immigrants headed to another land. Just like Sam, it takes courage to make it. And, as in the case of Salim Ziady, what awaits us is a new name, a new home, and a fresh start.

But first, step into the shoes of a young immigrant.

Don the cloak of courageous uncertainty.

And prepare yourself for a fascinating journey.

Max Lucado

Chapter One

The Early Days
in Lebanon

At the time of my birth, Beirut, Lebanon, was a beautiful and prosperous city, plentiful in history and culture. For hundreds of years, Beirut has been a center of business and trade for all the useful commodities and resources coming out of the Bekaa Valley and elsewhere in Lebanon. Situated in the middle of the civilized world, this ancient crossroads witnessed the movement of all the great civilizations as they passed through, extending and ruling their empires. From each, the land today known as Lebanon gleaned the newest developing technologies, political knowledge, and cultural and medical advances. Truly it was a place of destiny.

The Phoenician civilization settled here in ancient times, and later, Solomon found in our mountains the abundant cedars of Lebanon, the best timber in the known world, for his famous temple in Jerusalem. The Egyptians, the Greeks, the Romans, the Turks, and the French all came in turn.

This city of my birth was a well-respected center of commerce and culture during a time when other countries, especially in the New World, were neither settled nor discovered. Knives and forks, for instance, were in common use here when other parts of the world were still using crude tools made of stone. Dotted with beautiful villas, palm trees, and olive groves, the entire area around Beirut is an earthly paradise often referred to as "Paris on the Mediterranean" or "the Riviera of the Mideast." The city surrounds a breathtakingly beautiful horseshoe-shaped bay in the Great Sea.

Lebanon itself is about one hundred miles long and forty miles wide, occupying approximately four thousand square miles on the western shore of the Mediterranean. It is just north of Israel, with Syria on its eastern and northern borders.

I was born Salim Ziady in 1930, when Beirut was in the midst of a very peaceful and prosperous era under the French mandate. Swimming or skiing was available within an hour's drive. Wealthy tycoons and lords from around the Middle East came on leisurely holidays to enjoy the scenic beauty of the seashore and mountainous climate in this peaceful urban setting.

With all its progress, though, in some places in Lebanon, they still fish the way people did in Jesus' time. The net is cast out wide and the fishermen are spread out about a mile apart. Approximately five people on one side and five on the other slowly pull each end as they bring the net together. When they converge on shore, inside is a marvelous catch they call the "Old Mix." We would go to the docks and buy directly from the fishermen. How we loved eating those fresh fish.

Shortly after my birth, my father, Georgie, and mother, Mary, moved our family to Shuwayfat, where my paternal grandparents, Khalil and Housen Ziady, were living. In

Shuwayfat, a small village about six or seven miles from the city, our house was just a few doors down the street from where my grandparents lived. Today this whole area is one large metropolis and the former village has been swallowed up by the expansive growth of modern-day Beirut.

Precious Memories

My grandfather owned a large tract of land with beautiful olive groves. Many other families also lived on his land and worked for him. He had several agriculturally based businesses. From his olive orchards, he produced delicious oil the old-fashioned way—with a press. He also grew and manufactured carob syrup, which is a healthy and naturally sweet syrup folks used as a condiment. It tastes something like chocolate, and in America today it is used as a chocolate substitute. It is commonly served in the Middle East as a dip for bread, and is sometimes mixed with sesame syrup.

My grandfather was also in the soap business. He took the highly acidic olive oil and made it into soap. There are still a number of people throughout the world who buy this all-natural olive oil soap.

Grandpa started his life as a poor boy but he was very industrious and became a remarkably gifted businessman. He had both charisma and chutzpah and he was always a very honest man. After he was engaged to my grandmother, a most remarkable lady, she fell ill with smallpox. Her family came to Grandpa and told him, "You are free from your engagement because she is so sick. If she gets better she may look different or even be blind."

But he said, "Surely I will marry her." And it was never mentioned again. As it turned out, she didn't lose her sight and grandmother was a great blessing to my grandfather throughout his life, bearing him nine children: seven sons and two daughters. He lived happily, and his name and reputation were always well honored.

Grandfather passed away in 1931, when I was about a year old. And though I don't remember him, the picture I have in my mind is that he was always riding a white horse! A generous and kindly man, he was loved and respected in the village. In fact, the best daily catch of the local fishermen usually ended up on my grandfather's table because of his generosity to them.

Grandfather had been an only son who had several sisters. When he married my grandmother, the first two children to come along were the girls. Then came the seven boys. My father's two older brothers were rascals; they lived loosely and drank heavily. My father was the sober one, a good example to his four younger brothers. Father was a hardworking and wise son, my grandmother's favorite.

When I was born, I am told, my grandfather had a special affection for me. Most mornings he would come by our house and hold me on his lap and hug me. As far as he was concerned, the day didn't begin until he visited his grandson, the apple of his eye.

In 1929 the Great Depression came upon Lebanon. My grandfather had begun to borrow heavily from the bankers to avoid selling his oil and carob syrup at a loss, but the price never came back up during his lifetime. A wealthy man, he lost everything to those who had loaned him the money. Moreover, the local market for carob faded away for a time when everyone started using white English or French sugar instead. My grandfather's syrup spoiled and he lost that as well. Fortunately, they were able to keep the house, but that was about it. This reversal of fortune continually put him under a great strain and began to take its toll on his health.

Grandfather's Blessing

One day, sensing he had only a short time to live, he told my grandmother that he wasn't going to give his "blessing" to any of his sons, but rather to me, his favorite grandson. You will recall the biblical tradition of the blessing, where the patriarch of the family would invoke God's favor and care upon a child, usually the eldest son. Often the prayer would be that the son would know a life of consecrated service to the Lord and experience abundant prosperity and honor. He seriously charged my grandmother not to ever give his blessing to any of the other brothers or their sons. Grandfather gave me his blessing, and shortly thereafter he passed away.

Because I had received my grandfather's blessing when I was so little, it honestly didn't seem meaningful to me as I was growing up. I seldom even thought about it. I had no comprehension of its significance. It was only years later, when my grandmother gave Grandfather's special blessing to my new American-born son, that I realized its significance and importance. She recounted the tale of how Grandfather had instructed her to give his blessing to Sam's son. Little did she know then that I would go to America, marry an American girl, and then bring an American child back to her in Lebanon.

Even today, the cultural tradition in Lebanon is much the same as it was in biblical times. The birth of a first-born son is very significant. In years gone by, it was the sons who would eventually work the fields, fight the wars, and carry on the family name. Of all sons, the firstborn son was always the recipient of honor from all. For a king, the firstborn would one day become king himself. In the Scriptures the firstborn son enjoyed prominence and distinction (Ex. 4:22) and a double portion of the family inheritance (Deut. 21:15–17). Being firstborn also carried with it the responsibility to look after every other member of the family when the father died, and those duties began usually in childhood.

At the time of Joe's blessing, my grandmother was living with one of my uncles in Shuwayfat. It was a beautiful setting on a bright summer day. We were on the balcony overlooking the city below with the blue Mediterranean in the distance. My recollection is that those on hand were my mother and father, my uncle and his wife, Grandmother, Peggy, Joe, and myself.

Peggy could speak and understand very little of the Arabic language. She did realize the significance and solemnity of the occasion, though, when my grandmother covered her own head with a scarf, put her nine-month-old great grandson on her lap, and said,

> **My Great Grandson,**
>
> **May the God of Abraham, Isaac, and Jacob be with you and bless you. May your seed be blessed and prosper, may God's blessings of protection be upon you, may joy and peace be your portion.**
>
> **May the sun shine on you,**
> **May the wind be at your back,**

Whatever you touch, may it be as gold,
May your enemies be few and your friends be many.

Amen.

There wasn't a dry eye on the balcony that day.

When we visited Grandmother, she would always prepare a wonderful dinner for us. Mother was a great cook, but there was always something special about Grandmother's cooking. Whenever we went to see her, everyone always honored her by bowing, kissing her hand, and asking for her blessing. She was the matriarch of the family.

In the old country, the elderly were loved and respected. Never were they looked upon as a burden; always as a blessing to be cherished. Mine was a very happy life because my grandmother, uncles, and aunts all lived nearby. This was according to our custom.

Father and Mother

The reversal of fortune at the end of Grandfather's life was a very difficult turn of events. As a result, my father had to start his business from scratch, inheriting nothing from his father. This could have made him bitter, but he faced the challenge squarely and resolved to make a good life in spite of the setback.

My parents were good and loving people. Father and Mother loved each other dearly. Our family consisted of five boys and two girls, the oldest being myself, then Mike and Charles, then Ida, Tony, and Mouna, with Kelley being my youngest brother.

I remember my father as a hardworking and resourceful man whose various enterprises provided well for our needs. My mother was always at his side managing the family. After a while, they were able to set aside enough money to purchase a piece of land. My mother thought of a way to help Father with the expenses of our growing family. She planted a garden and raised Swiss chard, cauliflower, and spinach.

My dad and mom worked hard on this together, but she handled the money. My father would get up very early in the morning and take his mule into the city. He had a cart loaded with Mother's vegetables and he took them to the wholesale produce market and sold them to the merchants. He would come home holding a white handkerchief with the money folded inside. Mother used it to buy fabric. I can still see her sitting at her sewing machine for hours making shirts and other clothing for all of us.

My mother planted the seed of the love of God in all of us kids. My father was an honest man who believed in the principle of giving to Caesar that which is Caesar's and giving what is for God to God. He was not a regular churchman but he was always very principled. My mother was truly a devoted church-woman in the Eastern Orthodox tradition. She worshiped regularly at our nearby parish, St. Mary's. She would take us with her all the time. She loved the Lord, lived in a godly way, and prayed for the Lord to help her raise the family on a Christian foundation.

I remember going to church often with Mother at the age of three or four. One morning I was supposed to help her with my little brother Mike, who was about a year old. I was impressed even then with how Mother listened so carefully while the Bible was read by the priest. In Orthodox Christian tradition, everyone stands in reverence for the reading of the gospel.

After the Scriptures were read and the service was over, Mother went up to the front of the church where the priest was holding the Bible and she kissed the golden cover, thanking God for His blessed Word. Meanwhile I was holding on to my squirming little brother, waiting for her to return.

School Days

Mother found out about a missionary school that I could attend. She had met some Christian missionaries when I was about four. One of the missionaries, a Lebanese lady, knocked on our door and asked if Mother would like to send her boy to a small Christian school. By now, I had become almost hyperactive, and maybe this new atmosphere would help.

Mother asked her, "How much?"

The lady replied, "Fifty cents a month."

My mother smiled and told her, "If you want this little troublemaker for fifty cents, you can have him!"

Mother was glad to have a good place to send me where they would provide Christian training and trustworthy child care at the same time—two birds with one stone! Her hands were already full with my two little brothers, Mike and Chuck, and she was pregnant with my sister Ida. So it was helpful for her to have some relief in looking after me during the school day.

Miss Youmna Malek, who ran the school, was a very charming Christian woman who came from an Orthodox background. She had brought in some American missionaries to teach the boys and girls in the village about the Bible and also offer them a general education. It was here that I began to learn about America and the American culture for the first time.

Little did I know that later in life I would be publishing more Bibles than any man alive. When those missionaries came and knocked on our door, Mother was glad to see me go to a Christian school, but she had no idea what an impact it would have on all of us. Later, she was thankful that I could study with some of the best Bible scholars in America. Mother always loved the American people, and she wanted me to have an education there because she thought the Americans were absolutely the best in science and technology.

The Karrams were our next-door neighbors—good friends and good people. Elias, Alice, and Odette were older than I. Souheil was my age, and we went to kindergarten and first grade together. The night Mother gave birth to my brother Chuck, Souheil and I could not understand why she was locked up in her room with the midwife. Such serious talk was going on. We went outside and put a chair next to the window so we could climb up and see what was happening in her room. Souheil's oldest sister, Odette, saw us and chased us away. Both of us got a whipping for our mischief. We knew very little about babies and how they came into the world. (Of course, Souheil has never forgotten this event and he reminded me of it not long ago when we were having lunch in Boca Raton, Florida.)

It came as an awful shock when the Karrams, my closest friends, moved away to Jamaica. I was a young child, only six years old, but it seemed to me that life was no longer going to be any fun. It was the beginning of many changes I would have to face in the years ahead.

Back to Beirut

My father had accumulated enough money to move us back to the city. He wanted to be in Beirut because most of his business was there. We were again packing our bags, this time to move into a new two-story home my father had built. It had two apartments downstairs, and the upstairs, which was about 1,500 square feet, consisted of a couple of bedrooms, a living room, and a kitchen area. He had also put in a basement, which he used for storage. We rented out one of the downstairs apartments and lived upstairs. It was spacious and convenient, so my dad was very pleased with the move.

It was here that I started attending the new Christian evangelical high school just up the street from our house. When the new school year was beginning, Mother wanted to enroll us.

But my dad said, "There's not enough money." He was concerned that the tuition was a little beyond our reach. Mother offered, "I'll help out, Papa. I really want the kids to go to this school. It will be a lot better for them than the regular school, and they'll be right here within sight of the house." Father agreed because he knew Mother meant what she said about helping, and he also trusted her sound judgment in these matters. So we were enrolled.

Mr. Atchinak, our teacher and principal, and his wife, Asma Trad, who was also a teacher, were very strict, but always in a very loving way. For instance he insisted that if a child wanted to come to their school, that child would also have to be in Sunday school. There was a Muslim man, a colonel in the army, who told Mr. Atchinak, "I like your school but I don't like the Sunday school!"

One Sunday he kept his kids home. On Monday morning, when the man's kids came for school, Mr. Atchinak said, "Go home. No school for you today."

The Colonel was very upset. He showed up at the school later that day accompanied by soldiers from his platoon, and wanted to talk tough to Mr. Atchinak. But the principal told him, "Look, I make the rules. Perhaps you don't like it, but this is a *Christian* school. I started it, and I built it on the Word of God. So here it is: No Sunday school, no school."

It was there that we learned about salvation and being united with Christ. As a result of going to that school, I met many great Christian leaders, people like Dr. Lambie, Mr. Whitman, and a number of other missionary teachers who lived the Christian life to the fullest. This is where the Christian faith really took hold of me. We learned the New Testament, Old Testament, the stories of the great saints of God. We studied the life of Jesus Christ, His death and resurrection, the gift of salvation, and redemption. We read the Bible from cover to cover, and were always ready for pop quizzes. Every morning we began with devotions.

Years later, my brother Mike visited Mr. Atchinak after we had all grown up and gone into business. He said what he did at the school was "a call from God. I wouldn't do anything differently if I were to do it all over again. It would be the same." We all loved his single-mindedness. He was aggressive; he was tough. But we knew he loved us.

We students had been told to stay off a particular olive tree and not to jump on the branches. I was very high-strung and confident. And being mischievously disobedient was not unusual for me. One day I was jumping on the tree, and then hanging on the branch to show off. Then suddenly, I heard the bough breaking, and I fell to the hard ground below. I broke my arm in three places and suffered for my self-willed deed! They took me to the hospital, and I carried that heavy plaster cast around with me for two or three months. It was a hard lesson.

We had a math teacher there who was in a little over her head, and I was a strong student in math. While she was explaining the solution to a problem to the class one morning, I worked out the answer ahead of her and brought it to her desk. I knew I had nailed it, but she shoved it back to me and smirked. "You're wrong."

"I'm not wrong," I told her. Neither of us would back off. Then I said, "I'm going to the principal and show it to him."

She couldn't believe it when I returned and announced, "The principal said I'm right!" Later they downgraded her a couple of classes. I was more into right and wrong than I was into grace and mercy.

As the older brother, I was always very protective of my younger siblings. Mike got into a fight at school one afternoon while I was not around. He could usually take care of himself, but he was beaten pretty badly. When I heard about it, I ran like a panther chasing after the guys who had done this to him. I figured they must be bigger than usual for Mike to have taken such a licking.

When I caught up with the culprit, he was a boy much bigger than Mike or me. I got in his face and demanded, "Why did you beat up my brother?"

"I will beat you up too," he shot back.

I glanced at Mike first, and then I looked the bigger boy in the eye and said, "I'll show you." WHACK!

When I saw how badly his head was bleeding I knew that I would likely be punished too. The principal of the school, Mr. Atchinak, ran up and demanded, "Why did you do that?"

"It was self-defense. This guy really whipped my brother," I answered.

By now my mother was on the scene, and she came quickly to our defense, "My son didn't start it. I know my son."

This episode put the scare into the other kids. They wouldn't fight with any of my brothers anymore. I was their defender, and the word got around.

My competitive nature also began to show up in various games at school. We would play marbles, and I was determined to win. Mike and Chuck got into the habit of getting their marbles from my jar. I would ask them, "What did you do with my marbles?" I didn't really care because I had so many. They would lose them, and I would win them all back again.

I enjoyed playing soccer, too, and always to win. I was good enough to play with the upperclassmen, but not on the national level. My position was forward and I scored a lot of goals. They told me I was a good kicker and passer.

The sling I used for hunting gained me the reputation of being a good shot. One day I bagged seventeen fat birds, and we ate very well that night. When I got a little older, I learned to hunt with a shotgun. I loved to go out with my dad, and we frequently had fowl for dinner.

In the summer, Father would take us up into the mountains where the air was clearer and the weather cooler. We sometimes got up at four o'clock in the morning to climb to the top, where the altitude was about ten thousand feet. I can remember striving to make it to the summit first, looking down at the cedars of Lebanon. Somehow I'd been granted the will to win. Where on earth was I going to use it?

Chapter Two

The War Years

L ooking back, things began to change dramatically in 1939 when I was nine years old and World War II had broken out on a full scale.

I remember these were as dark years. The Vichy government in France, a puppet government supported by Hitler, was bombing the Free French forces in Beirut. There were air raids almost every night.

General Charles de Gaulle was heading the wartime government of the Free French. France had been overrun by Germany and de Gaulle made his headquarters in London, with many men garrisoned in Beirut. I remember seeing him visit on several occasions. The tall, lean Frenchman with his impressive entourage seemed almost godlike as he moved through the streets of the city. The traffic stopped and everything else came to a standstill as they passed by.

The Middle East seemed to be up for grabs. The forces of Hitler, Rommel, and Mussolini were moving in throughout the region. They had already occupied North Africa and were at the doorstep of Cairo.

The nights were black. No one was allowed to have lights on. We had to use small oil lamps and the windows had to be completely covered. In spite of our careful preparations, the enemy air force managed to come in almost every night with their dark gray planes and bomb the city. I remember the pilots were very daring. Their planes were fast, and they mercilessly dropped bombs all over the city: on the bridges, the amusement centers, and even on some schools and churches.

America had joined the Allied forces in the war. In addition to her troops, America became the greatest reservoir and supplier of ammunition and tactical equipment—airplanes, jeeps, food, and medical supplies—to the Allies. Most of the Lebanese people were relieved when America joined the war because of her wealth and strength. However, we in Lebanon were in a time of crisis because there were no supplies coming into the country. Rice and sugar were rationed, as were gas, oil, and tires. Only the wealthy were able to supply their families with the bare necessities of life.

One evening when the planes were bombing the city, I was sleeping in my bed next to the window. Not too far from our house was an ammunition depot. A plane was shot down and fell about one thousand yards from our house. It hit the ground and detonated the entire depot. The explosion was so great that most of the windows in our house were completely blown in and shattered.

Mother was already on her knees in front of a small candle-lit icon of Jesus Christ on the cross, with the Virgin Mary praying to the Lord for His protection. After the plane crash, Mother went through the house to make sure everyone was all right. My bed was covered with shards of glass.

The next morning, Mother gathered us all together. She told my father we should no longer stay in the city because it was not safe. We reluctantly realized the time had come to pack up and move to a safer location. Father borrowed a truck from one of his friends, and we packed what we could and took off to the mountains. There was about a month left of school. Mother made me bring my schoolbooks with me to study so I would not be behind when school opened again after the crisis.

Life in the Mountains

The house that we leased in the mountainous country was expensive—with so many people fleeing Beirut my father had to pay a premium for it. The man was glad to rent to us because he was a poor farmer. He thought we were rich people from the city, and perhaps by his standards we were. He moved into the basement where there was an extra room.

Not too far outside the door were his cows, goats, and sheep. There was a vineyard, too, and he made some of his own wine. He also had olive and fig trees. Although this house was not as nice as our city home, it was considerably better than most people were able to secure. It stood on a beautiful hill and not too far from it were stunning cliffs overlooking an expansive valley below.

In one of those cliffs was a small cave. Every day I took a little mat and a pillow into that cave. I would spend hours there reading. This was my first office—my little home away from home—although it was only about two hundred yards from the house.

The schoolbooks I brought with me to the mountains became a good excuse to get away for study and review. Of course, all the schools were closed. We knew we were going to be up in the mountains, in Aintoura above Dhoor el Shweir, for a while. It turned out to be four or five months. Mother did not want me to fall behind in my studies, so she insisted I read and reread all of the books I had taken with me. It gave me time to be by myself, free from the responsibility of baby-sitting my younger siblings and helping around the house.

By now, our family consisted of three boys and one girl. My sister Ida was not as healthy as we three boys. It seemed the war years took their toll on her. During the time we were exiled on the mountain, there were also a couple of doctors in the nearby village. We were blessed that we were only afflicted with minor illnesses. One way or another, God continually looked after us while we were hiding from the war.

In Lebanon, blue skies predominate most of the year, especially in late spring, summer, and early fall. However, in the mountains in the winter, there is much snow. We were not at a very high elevation, so it was quite a moderate climate—chilly at night, nice and sunny during the day—much like the weather in California here in the U.S.

Living out in the country, where we had palm trees, pomegranates, and fig trees all around the house, was extremely pleasant. A neighbor of ours had a small farm with sheep and goats. From him, my mother was able to buy enough food and milk to keep body and soul together. I remember how people came through from Syria and the Bekaa Valley and brought in beans, vegetables, and supplies. Mother would often purchase goods from them.

We three boys, Mike, Chuck, and I, were a team. I was always getting my brothers into trouble. I would get the worst of it from my father because, usually, I was the instigator of the mischief. One morning a trader came through our area. I was in the house and looked out and for the first time in my life saw a camel. Although I had seen them in pictures and movies, I had never seen one up close. The man actually had two camels and a donkey, and he tied them to a tree near the house.

While the trader was attending to selling his supplies, I loosened the ropes and jumped on one camel's back. When it got up from its knees, it took off like a rocket and I held on for dear life. The animal swayed back and forth as he sped on, and I was scared to death. I was at the verge of falling off. But before too long, the camel got tired of running with me on his back. God took pity on me, and the camel slowed to a stop.

My father was very unhappy with me when the report of my escapade reached his ears. He gave me a pretty good licking. It wasn't until many years later that I got on a camel again when I was visiting Jordan with my wife and my daughter Rachel. We rode camels as part of a special tour set up by our friends Shorty Yeaworth and Carolyn Horton. The tour took place where one of the scenes from *Lawrence of Arabia* was filmed. My second experience with a camel was much more enjoyable than the first!

My father would occasionally travel back down the mountain and into the city and see to his business interests. He had boarded up the windows of our house there, so it was closed up tight. But he would check on our belongings and call on some of his customers. He would sell the special soap made from olive oil for which the Ziadys were well known, and was able to get good prices because these things were now so scarce. From the profits he would supply the household with most of our needs. Because supplies were so limited, he had to get most of what we needed on the black market. This was expensive, but it was the only way to survive during the war.

In addition, he had about ten apartments from which he and Mother collected rent. With Mother's help they saved, built, and succeeded because they worked so very hard.

The Allies

After four or five months of living in the country, word came that Rommel had been defeated in North Africa. The Allied forces, especially those under Generals Montgomery and Clark, made their big move and succeeded in pushing the Germans and Italians back. I clearly recall going back to the city and seeing those wonderful Allied troops from England and Australia riding in their jeeps through the streets of Beirut. Our people were so glad to see them. With their arrival, food and gasoline became abundant again.

Although the war was still going on in other places in the world, in Lebanon we believed the Allies brought prosperity with them when they came. I couldn't help feeling a deep love and appreciation for the free way of life they represented. At age ten, I decided that one day I would visit America—especially after some of the missionaries had told me stories about Texas and how "great big" it was. "You can drive for one thousand miles and still be in the state of Texas," they told me. Just this one state was more than fifty times the size of Lebanon! I promised them, "If I ever get to America, I must visit Texas!"

Beirut was once again a city full of vitality, opportunity, beauty, and diversion. The stores were stocked with the goods of life. But unfortunately, parts of the city had become a hub of lascivious activity. The casinos and the hotels were wide open, busy at all hours. We had become an international city, a place for the playboys and the rich sheiks. In some ways Beirut had become the new "Sin City" of the Middle East.

When life returned to normal in 1941, I was ahead of my class because I had kept up with my studies during our time in the mountains. The school system in Lebanon was basically a French system. The first six years are called elementary or primary education. Students get a certificate when they have completed elementary school. After three more years, roughly the equivalent of seventh through ninth grades here in the States, a student earns a baccalaureate certificate for completing this intermediate level. Once that level is reached, you are ready to begin preparation for vocational studies such as engineering, medicine, or law. After vocational study, equivalent to eleventh and twelfth grades here in America, the foundation is laid to enter the university.

Because this school system is much more advanced, I was already ahead of students in the States in my age-group. Little did I realize how helpful this would be later on. Furthermore, the books I had studied in the mountains prepared me well, so I was a leg up on everyone else. As a result, I graduated from high school in 1945, valedictorian of my class.

The College of the Three Patriarchs

Shortly after my graduation, I enrolled at the College of the Three Patriarchs, the flagship of the schools in Beirut and the official college of the Orthodox Church in our area. This was preparatory for entry into a profession such as law or medicine, and I was leaning toward medicine.

The man who is now Patriarch Ignatius IV of Antioch, who oversees all the Antiochian Orthodox archdioceses worldwide (he lives on the "street called Straight" in Damascus, as mentioned in Acts 9:11), taught literature and sports at this school. He has brought wonderful spiritual renewal to the Orthodox Church today. I remember him as a good and honest man and an effective coach, especially in soccer. I improved in soccer, thanks in part to his patient and thorough work.

We called him Pére (Father) Hazim. As teachers go, he was a little more reserved than most. He loved the students, though, and would go the extra mile to help us. But if we weren't serious, we were on our own! He taught Mike and Chuck as well.

Pére Hazim did not pastor a parish, but was an assistant priest in a parish not too far away. His work at the church's school was his primary assignment. In the old country an Orthodox priest could be married before ordination if he wished. This is one of the major differences in practice between the Roman Church and the Orthodox Church. If a priest does decide to marry, he usually settles in to pastor a parish. A young seminarian is generally not assigned a parish unless he is married.

If a priest has dedicated his life to celibacy, he is eligible to one day become a bishop within the church. Sometimes these specially dedicated young clergy go into archdiocesan administration, work in education and study for further degrees, or specialize in ministry to the poor. Some may even enter the monastic life. Pére Hazim was such a celebate priest.

My years at the Three Patriarchs were not easy. There were many long nights of study. All exams were on a competitive basis, and everything was graded on a curve. A student's standing in the class meant everything with regard to his future, because the universities selected only the highest ranked. If you missed out, you could not enter the respected professions, which would provide you with better than average income throughout your life.

A Turn for the Better

By this time, at age sixteen, I began to realize how tough life would be if I did not take advantage of a good education. I pondered my future, and I began to think more seriously about God. A new awareness of the Lord was brought upon me by a neighbor, a strong Christian believer. Every morning he would fall on his knees and pray. This used to bother me a great deal. He frequently told me, "The only way you will get to heaven is by truly following Jesus Christ."

This man lived in the small, first-floor apartment of our two-story house. His name was Jad Hatim. Brother Jad was a man in his forties. He worked as a peddler, selling cloth goods for a living. He was poor but very happy. You could hear him singing hymns to the Lord every morning. He became a

Christian through the efforts of American missionary workers, and he was a godly example for me. He was an active member in a nearby church, sharing the gospel with his neighbors and seeing to the needs of those in prison.

I had been baptized as an infant, and I knew being born again meant separation from the world. But I had been having too much fun to live a life consecrated to Christ and centered in the church. Thank God I never went too far astray or off the deep end. My father, my brothers, and I were sympathetic to Christianity, but the Bible did not mean very much to me, and I did not have a living fellowship with God. My biggest concern was to do well in school, and I was becoming interested in being a good doctor. I wanted to postpone living as a Christian until I was older and settled.

But God had a plan for me. I had an awakening.

Very early one morning in late 1947, I had taken my double-barreled 12-gauge shotgun down from the rack and was going out to hunt ducks. As I was making my way toward the river, I saw a man dressed in a dark suit lying on the ground. As I got closer to him, my knees began to tremble. I was horrified. He had been shot. I saw blood coming out of his ears. He felt cold. Then I looked again at his face and realized I knew him. It was the biggest shock of my life.

Although the man came from a nice home, the first thought that came to my mind was that he had died and did not have any time to get right with God. That awful moment was my awakening to Christ. I took this crime as a direct call from God to me. This was a personal warning that the wages of sin is death. This also was a warning for anyone who dies without Christ, that they will face eternal judgment. What a stern reminder this was to me from a loving heavenly Father.

Of course, I was so bothered that morning that I did not go hunting. I came back home and wanted to talk to my neighbor, Jad, about God. But he was not there. So I stayed around the house all day, nervously trying to read the Bible.

Finally, I heard him singing down at the end of the street. I rushed out to meet him, grabbed him by the arm, and said, "Brother Jad, I want to become a real believer."

I told him my story of the death of my friend and my subsequent decision to become a dedicated Christian. He couldn't believe his ears. He and I got down on our knees on an old rug right there in his apartment, and I gave my life to Jesus Christ as the Lord and Master of my life. Things took a new turn. A fresh chapter was opened in my life. I had a wonderful awareness that my name was written in the Book of Life.

For several months I did not know what to do next. I started reading the Scriptures and trying to evaluate God's will for me.

My First Crack at Business

At the end of 1948, I decided to drop out of college. Dad told us he couldn't afford to cover the tuition for all of us anyway. So we boys came up with a plan.

Instead of using the money available to pay for tuition, we made an agreement with Father to invest the sum in a grocery store. Mike and later Chuck were my partners, and we all worked very hard to keep things running right. The store was so prosperous that we were able to cover their tuition needs plus have some extra money. I was also able to put away some money for myself that I eventually used to come to America. We sold family specialties: olives, olive oil, carob syrup, our specialty soap, and produce such as beans, cauliflower, and spinach.

I bought the supplies and the canned goods. Then I added 5 percent to the cost so Mike, who was selling these goods, would not sell them too cheap or at cost. Mike was a good salesman. He moved the inventory well and made a good profit. Chuck started to help us, and he became a good manager. It was called the Ziady Brothers Store, and my father was very proud. By the time I left for America, they were running two locations.

During this period of my renewed Christian life, I met Dr. Tom Lambie, a missionary and medical doctor from Pennsylvania who was working in Jordan. He had been a professor of medicine at the University of Pennsylvania before coming to the Middle East. His brother-in-law happened to be Dr. Robert McQuilkin, president of Columbia Bible College in South Carolina.

This tall, impeccably credentialed man in his fifties had come to Beirut on his way to Bethlehem to build a hospital for the refugees in the Holy Land. (To reach Bethlehem in those days, it was safer to enter via Beruit.) I got to know him through my school when he came to speak.

After Dr. Lambie spoke to the class, I went up to say hello. He had a car he was bringing in from America to drive to Bethlehem with supplies. I helped him get his things through customs—I was good at getting those kinds of things done. We became friends quickly, and he gave me a lot of good advice. Dr. Lambie was a committed and sincere Christian. He was also a wonderfully kind man, and genuinely interested in me.

I told him about my commitment to Christ and the uncertainty I still felt about my future plans. I said, "I'm not sure what to do with my life. I want to be a doctor and would like to go to a good school like Harvard or Yale." I had been thinking very seriously about either going to medical school or becoming a businessman, and I wanted to go to America and attend a top school. But I didn't have enough money.

We met together often during his visits, and on one occasion he gave me a copy of a book by George Müeller called *The Life of Faith*. I read the book in one sitting, and it had a tremendous impact on me. The story is about how George Müeller saw all his prayers answered except one. He had prayed for his brother's salvation for years. Finally, nearing death, his brother became a Christian.

This is a powerful story of prayer and faith. That book greatly inspired me. I was eighteen years old when I read it, and as a result I surrendered my life to God in an even deeper way. I got on my knees and said, "God, if You will do for me what You did for Müeller, I'll put my hand in Your hand and You will carry me all the way through."

I've had some terrible times and some bad setbacks since. When all hell would break loose, I would get on my knees and say, "God, You're still on the throne, and I know things are tough right now, but please, You've got to help me!" That book radically changed my life.

Dr. Lambie told me, "I think you should go to school in America, and I know God can use you." He felt God was dealing with me, and he wanted me to find His will. He added that it would be a good idea to attend a Christian college first to become grounded in the faith, and also to find work. He suggested Columbia Bible College in South Carolina and offered to be my guardian. He worked it out with Dr. McQuilkin to be my sponsor. So if I could get the nod from my father, I could go to America with my life savings of $600.

Talking It Out

Here I was, a young man pursuing medical studies who had just become a truly committed Christian six months earlier. Now I was wanting to go to America, but I had only $600 to my name.

My father was opposed to it. I was his number one son. He didn't want the eldest to leave. He had seen it all too often: When the first son left, they all left, following him. He and Mother would wind up with nobody home. This is the story of the families of Lebanon. Furthermore, I was educated, and he needed me to stay and help build his business.

But I had my eyes on America. I had an adventurous spirit, and having met all these American missionaries who told me their stories, I wanted to see America for myself.

I still wasn't sure what God had planned for me. It would have to be a step of faith completely. Did I still want to be a doctor? That's what my earlier dream was. Sometimes I thought I would rather be a businessman—or maybe even a missionary like Dr. Lambie. I prayed, "Lord, I want to be whatever You want me to be. I put my faith in You. I want to trust You, one step at a time, one day at a time."

In the beginning my father's opposition to my going was quite harsh. He insisted I stay in Beirut and help him build his business. His ten apartments were paid for by this time, and they were earning him nice profits. He was willing to mortgage them and add the capital to our grocery business, with me in charge.

He said to me, "You are the eldest, the leader of the family, and I need you to stay here with me and your brothers—to take over the business for me. It would be a waste to just let it go. You have a good business mind, and you could become very successful."

When he saw I wasn't being persuaded he took an even harder line. "You can't go. You don't have any money. You have a home here you live in, and you don't pay any rent. You've got a beautiful future. Why do you want to mess all that up and go to America? You don't have anybody over there—no brother, sister, aunt, or uncle. Where are you going to go?"

I just looked at the floor.

He finally added, "Where is your common sense? You don't know anything. You are just nineteen. Listen to me. I've been there. I know."

I said, "Dad, you don't understand."

"What don't I understand?" he asked. "I'll send you to medical school here."

"I just want to go for a trip," I replied. "I'll come back."

Dad warned, "A little trip. You don't have much money.

You will spend your savings on a fare over there and then come back broke. I want you to know I'm not going to send you any money. I can't support you in America."

I said, "Dad, you don't have to support me."

"The only money I'll send you is a ticket to come back," he continued.

I countered, "Don't worry. God is sending me over there, and He is going to supply all my needs."

Raising his eyebrows, he answered, "We'll see."

Final Arrangements

A couple of weeks later, after we had both cooled off, Mother said to my father, "Don't fight it. He is going to go. He has made up his mind."

We didn't want to keep having a war so we tried to make peace. Dad cried and said, "I hate to see you leave. You are making a mistake. I love you. May God go with you. Write to us. And don't forget, we want you back."

I had to make arrangements for a visa, but I didn't actually have a birth certificate. So I went to the priest, and he asked me how old I was.

In the old country the priest is the official record keeper of one's birth. The old priest was there when I was born, and another baptized me. Our current priest wasn't either of those. The old priest who baptized me had passed on. So things were not firmly nailed down as to when I was actually born.

I was baptized in the church, and they had an undated record of it, but you can be baptized at the age of six months or fifteen months or two years—so who knew for sure? We didn't have an actual record of my birth, but I got my visa without any trouble.

I borrowed enough money from my father to buy a ticket, about $700. I had the $600 I had saved from my grocery store, so when I arrived in America that would be my net worth. I was coming here against my father's best wishes, but God had opened the doors.

Chapter Three

Coming to America

I was nineteen years old when I obtained my visa to come to the United States. My ticket was on Air France to fly to New York. At that time Air France had some of the largest planes flying internationally. I was booked on the legendary DC-6, a four-engine prop plane that seated approximately 150 people.

When we took off from Beirut on August 10, 1950, I was hoping to arrive in New York approximately August 15. In those days the DC-6 made stops in Cairo, Paris, and Shannon, Ireland, before reaching New York City. In Cairo, however, we had some problems with the plane. One of the engines wasn't working properly, and we were told we would have to wait for another plane. Since my name was Ziady and Z is the last letter of the alphabet, I was last in line to resume my journey. Most of the passengers got on board and continued their travels, but I was stuck in Cairo.

Actually, "stuck" puts a worse face on it than is necessary. It turned out to be a completely wonderful turn of events. I was in Cairo about a week, all at the expense of Air France. Then after completing the next leg of my trip, I had to lay over another seven or eight days in Paris—again at the expense of Air France!

Being fluent in Arabic and French, I had a great time in both places. I felt all of these serendipitous disruptions were presents to me from God. For instance, in Cairo I knew a young fellow studying to become a doctor. When I called I found out this just happened to be the two weeks between semesters for him, so we spent almost the entire time together. We hit the Cairo zoo, various museums, and visited the Pyramids. He shared that entire city with me in a way that few foreign visitors would ever be privileged to experience.

The stay in Paris was even better, though I was alone there. I walked the Champs Élysées, visited the tomb of Napoleon, Versailles, the Eiffel Tower, the Arch de Triumph, as well as Fountainebleau, the famous residence of Louis XIV. It was all so beautiful and fantastic. I was using my French for the first time in the heart of France, and I found I had no problem making myself understood. It was an extraordinary visit, courtesy of the airline. When God offers a present like this, you feel His power and love in a way that you remember for the rest of your life.

Nevertheless, I was somewhat concerned about my delay in getting to Columbia Bible College. The first semester began at the end of August. I had been hoping to arrive two or three days ahead of schedule, knowing I would need some time to adjust to American culture and the educational system, which was new to me. But with all the time I spent in Cairo and Paris, I didn't arrive at Idlewild Airport in New York City until September 8, a Friday. With that, my life in America began.

I had heard many stories about the American people: They are tough and strong; they are very attached to the land; and they are great hunters, fishermen, and sportsmen. The cities were portrayed as gargantuan, and with all the lights, the night was as bright as the day. Some of this came from the Hollywood movies I had seen, and some of it was, I suppose, just folklore I had picked up along the way.

I was also eager to learn about what Americans ate. I didn't know much about the food, but I knew the American people seemed a little heartier than the Europeans. And I had picked up that they were perhaps a little less cultured or civilized, but definitely more adventurous—especially those living out in the country. I was very, very excited to finally have arrived on American soil.

By now it was early evening, about 7:00 or so. The bus from the airport had taken an hour to get into the city, and I was lucky to get a seat in the back. It was crowded and hot, and I hadn't slept well on the flight from Ireland. But I was so excited; I guess I was running on adrenaline.

You need to understand, my English was very limited during those first few days. I might have had a working vocabulary of about four or five hundred words. However, if one speaks French, many of the words are very similar to English, and some are identical except for the pronunciation. Somehow I found my way over to the Atlantic Hotel in midtown Manhattan, at about 38th Street and Sixth Avenue.

I had heard that Americans ate all kinds of things, and I wanted to walk the streets of New York and have my first American meal. I saw a sign that said SANDWICH. That's a French word, too, and it's spelled exactly the same in both languages. I walked over to the sidewalk counter and stood in line. Right beside me people were streaming out of a theater where the movie had just finished. I was busy taking it all in. Suddenly I realized the guy with the little paper cap was pointing to the menu behind him and asking me, "What do you want?"

I saw the sign HOT DOG. I knew what the word *hot* meant and knew what the word *dog* meant. Then I saw those wieners rolling on the cooker, and I thought to myself, *No! It can't be. These crazy Americans.* I could hardly believe my eyes! I had heard that Americans ate bear, deer, and rabbit, but I never dreamed they would eat dog meat like the Chinese.

The man was a typical New Yorker—nervous and impatient—and he was cajoling me: "Come on, man, what do you want?"

I quickly told him, "Coca-Cola."

Through the Eyes of an Immigrant

I had also heard about the Empire State Building. So while sipping my drink I decided to see for myself if it was as big as it was reported to be. Everyone I had ever spoken with about New York City and its landmarks told me it was over a hundred stories tall. But frankly, I did not believe them. I thought, *This is just a bunch of American propaganda. I've got to go see it.*

So I walked down to 34th Street and when I got close to the corner, I looked up and saw a building so tall that I couldn't even count all the way to the top. I got mixed up each time I tried. Finally, I visually divided the building in half so I could count it from the halfway point down without losing my place.

From halfway down it came to about fifty stories. I said to myself, "Sure enough, those crazy Americans, they're right."

After walking a few more streets and seeing the crowds and the neon signs of Times Square, it was all like a dream coming to life. By the time I headed to my room at the hotel, I was exhausted, but so excited I did not sleep well. I got up the next morning and had breakfast: a boiled egg, ham, cheese, and coffee. By ten o'clock in the morning I was on the shuttle bus again, headed out to La Guardia to catch my flight to Columbia, South Carolina. I was wearing a big, double-breasted suit and a large, light-colored hat.

Welcome to CBC

Finally I landed in Columbia, South Carolina. That was the end of my long trek from Beirut. Two seniors from the college were waiting to greet me and help me get to the school. The three of us made our way across campus, and I was assigned to my room. It was a corner room with two single beds. Each bedroom was adjoined by a small room with a washbasin and a commode, and each floor of the dorm had a shower room with four or five stalls. I remember the wooden floors in the rooms were painted brown.

The first night in Columbia was rainy and foggy. After two weeks it seemed it rained all the time there. Lebanon gets only one-third of the rainfall that South Carolina gets annually, but the bulk of the rain in Beirut comes during only three or four months. In South Carolina it just comes all the time.

My new roommate was Jack Hayes. It turned out his circumstances were special too. He had already taken a semester or two elsewhere, and now he was coming to Columbia. Jack was kind, thoughtful, and pleasantly laid back. He was there more or less to please his mother. We were opposites, but friends, and it worked out well.

I learned he was from Charlotte, North Carolina, and that he attended the Calvary Presbyterian Church in Charlotte where Billy Graham's mother and the whole Graham family attended. Jack's father had been a colonel in the army, and after that he became a sales manager with the local Ford agency in Charlotte. They lived in a very nice home, and Jack had me over during the holidays and on an occasional weekend. It meant a lot to me to have Jack and his family as close friends.

My classmates, the other guys on the floor, were great to get to know. Earl McWay was easygoing, determined, disciplined, a contented student, and an uplifting example. Bob Williams, next door, was a fireball and wanted to change the world. Dick Basso from Vermont was consistent, but had no special long-term ambition or goals, as I recall. Bob Yount from Michigan was steady, happy, in love with Betty (whom he later married), had strong goals, and never worried about money. Keith Hood was from England, and Chanda Pella was from India—a very serious and reserved student.

My second night on campus the school was having a welcoming party sponsored by the sophomores for the new freshman class. Wouldn't you know it, they were serving hot dogs! I wanted to ask Jack about it. You can't just ask anybody you meet a question like that, but he was my roommate, and I felt I could trust him. After the freshmen were introduced to the sophomores, I just flat out asked him, "What is a hot dog made of?"

Jack smiled kindly and said, "I don't think even the United States government knows what hot dogs are made of." I have never been a great fan of hot dogs and still am not to this day.

At the party the girls were friendly to me and to the other boys. Girls in America seemed happier and more outgoing, more expressive, and they dressed more casually in public than girls in the old country. I was shy and backward around them.

Meeting Billy Graham's Mother

After being in America for about four months, I went with Jack to his home for a weekend visit. We drove to Charlotte, and it was there I had the opportunity to meet Billy Graham's mother, Morrow. She was fascinated with me and my story. What a gracious lady. She extended her love to me and said she was going to be praying for me. Little did I suspect that in just twelve short years she would become one of the early investors in my company, and that her prayers would be answered in ways neither of us could then imagine.

Mrs. Graham impressed me as a godly woman. She loved to read the Bible and still lived out in the country on a farm where Billy Graham was raised along with the rest of the family. He had become a strong, well-liked evangelist in the church at large, and I was hoping I could meet him at his mother's house, but we never did see him there. I didn't personally meet him until many years later.

We lived on the second floor of Legster's Hall at CBC. One Sunday after church I was in my room, lying on the bed, resting a moment before going over to the school dining hall for Sunday dinner. A good friend, Elmer Towns, stopped by my room, and I got up to visit with him. While we were talking the guys in the room above mine were roughhousing. Suddenly, all the plaster on the ceiling above me let go and covered my bed and part of the bed next to it. This was a building constructed in 1830, and the ceiling was inch-thick heavy plaster. If I had been on the bed, I doubt it would have killed me, but I would most likely have been hurt. I thank the Lord, who spared me that day by sending Elmer Towns by for a visit.

The food at CBC was quite different from what I had been accustomed to in Beirut. Back home, a typical breakfast would consist of hard-boiled eggs, olives, yogurt, pita bread, jellies, and hot tea. Here they served grits, soft eggs, bacon, cereal, and fruit. I took a liking to the cereal and fruit right away, but had a harder time learning to eat the grits. At first I added sugar to get them down, but later I adjusted to them. In the old country we ate lots of lamb, beef, and fish. In South Carolina we were served pork, chicken, and casseroles. Some food had a strange taste to me, so once in a while I went to bed a little hungry.

Learning English

Dr. Robert McQuilkin was the college president and my sponsor. He called and asked me to come see him. We talked for a while about our friend and my guardian, Dr. Lambie. Then we spoke at length about my new situation at Columbia Bible College. He carefully covered each area where I might have needs or questions.

Dr. McQuilkin said he would be glad to assist me in any way he could. I knew he sincerely meant what he said, so I told him the one thing I needed most was help with my English. I knew I would not be able to do my studies satisfactorily with the little bit of English I knew. He agreed and saw to it that I was enrolled in a remedial English course. He also said that if I needed a job, he had an opening in the kitchen—washing dishes.

I thought I would be the only student in remedial English, but I found there were more than a dozen students who were native English-speaking Americans taking this class too. It was a noncredit course and simply an opportunity to bring our skills in English up to a level of competency that would enable us to work at the college level. It helped me get the jump start I needed. The teacher went out of her way—a wonderful lady— in trying to instruct us. She took great pains to cover some of the more difficult items such as synonyms, adjectives, irregular verbs, sentence structures, and word pronunciations. This was a huge help. God was even in the little details, preparing me for the future.

My first regular class was a basic course in history. But I was allowed to read the material in French! This all came about thanks to Prof. George Dollar. He hit upon the idea that if he could test me in French on material I'd read in French, then he could give me a grade that would count the same as if I had studied and been tested in English.

St. Valentine's Day

The evening before Valentine's Day, I noticed a lot of the young men on campus were very busy. I did not know anything about Valentine's Day or its meaning. I saw the guys getting gifts for the girls—candy, flowers and cards. They told me the next day everyone would be dressed in their Sunday best.

One of my classsmates suggested I find a girl and let her be my valentine. I was still very shy and wasn't about to ask a girl I did not know to go out with me. I had not been in this country long enough to feel at ease in things like that.

One of the guys in the dorm said there was a nice girl who did not have a boyfriend. "You tell her, 'I'll be your valentine if you'll be my concubine.'" I didn't know what either word meant, but I suspected the worst when the girl was about to slap me. The guy who tricked me had a good laugh at my expense. The girl knew I could not speak English very well, so she forgave me. There are things we immigrants must learn the hard way.

Living on campus and meeting so many American kids augmented my learning tremendously. It seemed as if I were caught up in a tornado, and I had to learn to pick up things very quickly. The first semester I took only four credit hours in history. But by the end of the second semester, I had picked up fourteen credits with passing grades in all of them.

Paying the Bills

Second semester, my money began to run out. The $600 cash reserve I brought with me from Lebanon was running low, and I had to find a good-paying job. Dr. McQuilkin had given me my first employment, washing dishes in the cafeteria kitchen. Of all the things I could choose to do, this work would be last on my list! I hated those long hours working in the hot kitchen, and I was earning only forty-five cents an hour.

So I moved up in the world. I took a job making fifty-five cents an hour at the Shell station a block from school. Back then gas was twenty cents a gallon. Somebody would come in, fill up on two or three dollars' worth of gas, and I would have to clean the windshield, check the air in all four tires, and make sure the oil was up to the right level—all for a two-dollar purchase. It was a hopeless situation. At the end of the day my fingernails would be stained a greasy black. This was better than washing dishes, but I knew neither of those jobs was going to give me the kind of money I needed to finance my education.

Working, going to school, and studying didn't leave much time for fun, but we did manage to get a little recreation. One of the things I enjoyed the most was when we would get a bunch of the guys together on the basketball court. I had never played the game. I had to learn how to dribble, shoot, and pass the ball. What a great workout! We would get all sweaty and tired, then take a shower and go back to studying feeling much better.

I kept looking for a better job. A fellow named Ted Laws, who was in charge of cleaning the floors at the Colonial Food Stores, asked if I would like to work for him. He said he'd pay seventy-five cents an hour. They had a floor-polishing machine with rotary brushes, and I had to learn to hold it securely and direct it back and forth. I worked from 4:00 or 5:00 in the afternoon until about 8:00 or 9:00 in the evening, and again on Saturdays. It wore me out, but it got me through the year. I earned enough to finish school, but I was flat broke by the end of May.

School was not easy. Most of the professors graded on a curve, and somebody was always getting everything almost perfect and ruining it for everyone else. I managed to make Cs at first but then started to make an occasional B. I was glad to finish my first year with passing grades.

Toward the end of the semester I was constantly preoccupied with the financial obligations facing me, for the current school year as well as the next. My money had run out. I started pouring my heart out to God, praying on my knees and asking Him, "How can I make the kind of money I need, Lord? What kind of work can I do that will cover my expenses? I need Your help to find a well-paying job for the summer."

I took God at His word. He "shall supply all your need according to His riches in glory" (Phil. 4:19 NKJV). And I kept reminding Him of my needs.

Chapter Four

That Memorable
First Summer

My boss from the floor-polishing job at Colonial had patiently listened as I worried out loud about my finances over a couple of months. He was going to be interviewing some kids to sell books door-to-door during the summer and asked if I would be interested. I said I would, and he arranged an interview.

Two young men with crew cuts came to campus to speak with interested students. They explained it was an internship program during the summer break from school, selling Bibles, dictionaries, and Bible storybooks door-to-door. When I first considered it, I felt that with my broken English and heavy accent I probably couldn't sell very successfully. I knew, too, that around strangers I was by nature very shy. Nevertheless, my competitive side took over. I decided to take it to the next step and find out all that I could about the opportunity.

When I showed up for the second interview, there were a couple of new guys from the company and some of the students who had sold books the summer before. They were already signed up to do it again. The interviewers showed me a big family Bible and explained that it sold for $29.95. I thought to myself, *It's got to be pretty hard to sell a Bible for $29.95—that's almost a week's pay!* Then I asked them, "How many of these Bibles do you sell?"

One of the student managers assured me, "We sell a whole lot of them."

I looked around the room and asked no one in particular, "How much money did you make last summer?"

One of the kids stood up and said, "I made $2,200," and he showed me a copy of his check. I couldn't believe it! The other student manager said, "I made $2,740, and a number of the guys made even more."

Holy smoke!, I thought. *If I could make half of that in a summer I would be delighted.* Room and board and tuition at Columbia Bible College at that time totaled about $1,000 for the whole year.

So I signed up to be a salesman. I recalled seeing a sign in the window of a gas station that read: SIX MONTHS AGO I COULDN'T SPELL SALESMAN. NOW I IS ONE. Suddenly it wasn't quite as funny as it had been the first time I saw it. That was exactly what I was facing. With such broken English, I was signed up to be a salesman for the summer.

They had us go to sales training school. Each of the sales managers had several student managers under him, and each student manager had three to five salesmen. They were responsible for being sure their students not only knew the demonstration by heart but also how to overcome objections. We stayed until midnight learning the sales talk. I had memorized my routine before sales school started, but it needed refining. And I needed lots of encouragement from the managers!

My assignment was to work with a seasoned manager in Sumter, South Carolina, for most of the summer. It was a small town, maybe twenty thousand people, or even less. There was a large air force base there called Shaw Airfield. It was a training facility for U.S. Air Force personnel, and it was also a backup base for nearby Fort Jackson, a large training base for the army.

In Sumter I bought a used bike for ten dollars. I put my sample case and books up on the handlebars, and I would go through the neighborhoods, up and down back streets, wherever I could find people who would open the door and listen to me.

We divided the city into sections, and we all knew which streets were ours to work. We covered them in methodical order so we would not skip any homes.

Opening Day!

My first day selling was just like any other day; the sky was blue, and the weather was not too hot. It was early June. I was very nervous. I picked up my sample case and started knocking on the first door. Nobody was there. At the second door, a young girl answered. She wanted to know what I had for sale. I told her and asked if she would like me to show her the Bible. She said, "Yes."

We went inside and sat down. I started showing her the Bible with great zeal. I was eager to see if I knew my demonstration well, and if I would be able to close the sale. She reacted very well, especially to my accent.

She said, "Please come back. I know my daddy will buy that Bible if you come back Saturday." I promised her I would. I took his name and the phone number and thought to myself, *This is going to be my first sale.*

At the third house an elderly lady came to the door, and I showed her the Bible. But it was too big and heavy. Besides, she would probably have liked to own a Bible with large print, but we didn't have a giant print Bible. She said she was happy with her present Bible, but I made a good presentation to her. I was beginning to get the hang of it.

Nobody was at the fourth house, but next door was a nice, freshly painted house with flowers all around it. When I walked toward the front step, I saw this big gray German shepherd. I looked at him, and he looked at me and started growling. I backed away, holding my briefcase out in front of me. I was thinking, *If he comes at me, he's going to get that briefcase in his mouth before he gets me.* I was sure he would not be interested, and I had no German edition to offer him anyway.

I went from house to house all day long and did not sell one single product—not a Bible, not a Bible storybook, not a dictionary.

Throughout the week I had visited a number of homes, but in so many cases the people who answered the door explained they could not make this kind of a decision. Several told me if I could come back on Saturday when their husband would be home, then I could make my presentation directly to someone who could actually purchase the Bible. I thought Saturday was going to be my big day. I was hoping to make $100, but I didn't make a single sale.

At the end of the week, I had only managed to sell one

Bible storybook and one Bible. My total profit for that week was less than twenty dollars. I knew I could be making more money flipping hamburgers than I was selling Bibles. By Saturday night, I was in despair. What had I gotten myself into?

The Pep Talk

On Sunday afternoon we had a sales meeting. I was still down in the dumps, grumbling about how I had made more money washing dishes or cleaning floors. The manager directed his comments to me. "The reason you haven't sold much is because you didn't show the books strongly enough. You didn't explain the benefits of the Bible to the customer."

Actually, he almost preached me a sermon. He really busted my chops.

"All these people you call on are making enough money to make payments on TVs, cars, and everything else they have," he continued. "And you let them tell you they can't afford to put a five-dollar deposit on a Bible?"

Then he said something to me I've never forgotten. "Take the *N* and put it behind the *O*. When the customer says 'NO,' it means go 'ON' and show them more benefits, help them to better understand how this Bible will benefit each person in the family, especially the children." Suddenly, I began to get the picture. I started to feel stronger, more confident. Okay, I would be more forceful with the customers.

The next week I began to go at it much harder, and I started to close more sales. I made seventy-one dollars at the end of that second week. While that was a big improvement, it still wasn't enough money to go to school on.

We stayed in a small rooming house. I paid about six dollars a week, and my roommate also paid six dollars a week. We went to church in the area. It was a grueling pace. I usually started about 8:30 in the morning and wouldn't give up until about 9:30 in the evening. These were long, hot days. Many times I inadvertently awakened people. I was cussed at and thrown out of homes because people were asleep or annoyed at the interruptions.

Eating meals was something I just tried to fit in as best I could. At lunchtime I would feel hungry and grab a hamburger or some other kind of sandwich and a Coke. I would eat what I could, something inexpensive and fast. As the early evening came, I would be focused on my selling and hardly ever thought about food until I interrupted a family during their supper.

Frankly, people were often very gracious. Many times when I interrupted their meal they would invite me to join them. This was especially kind. Where else would I have gotten a nice free home-cooked meal? I think it was pleasant for the people, too, extending their generosity and finding out about a kid from Lebanon selling books and Bibles in South Carolina.

I loved being with the families with kids. They would always be very curious about me and interested in how I came to this country. Sometimes they were more interested in hearing about the old country than in seeing my Bibles. I had to increase my efforts to talk more about the Bible and less about Lebanon.

The third week I was determined to do still better. My skills seemed to get stronger with each presentation. By the end of the third week I had made $142. The boss said to me, "See how much more you made? And you still can make more than that if you'll put more effort into it."

He counseled me, "Don't waste time on customers who aren't interested in buying. Be sure to make enough demonstrations each day. Decide on how many demonstrations you're going to make and don't quit until you have completed them." The game plan was to make enough demonstrations to qualified customers and to convince them of all the benefits of the books.

By August I had shown great improvement. Week by week, as the hours and days flew by, I had saved $2,685! That was far more money than I had ever dreamed I could earn. God had answered my desperate prayers more abundantly than I would dared to have asked. Of course, I kept my expenses very low. I don't think I spent $250 that whole summer. I even washed and ironed my own clothes.

Toward the end of the summer my deliveries went very well. I was so happy, and I couldn't believe that I had saved that kind of money. But God had given me even more than the financial security I needed for the next school year. He had taught me that honest, hard work was good, and that taking a chance with something new could yield big returns.

It all worked together. My skills in English had improved greatly over the summer, and I now had a focused sense of purpose in my life. God could and would use me. He would show me what my gifts were, and I would be able to do great things with His help and guidance. But I had to be willing to give Him everything I had.

The Chevy

Once I got back to school one of the first things I did was to pay my tuition and room and board—$985 for the entire year. After that I had $1,700 left, in $100 bills. I had ridden my bike all summer. Now what I had on my mind was a car. This was part of the American dream for me.

I biked over to Central Chevrolet on Gervais Street, not far from campus. I was talking to one of the salesmen, but he wasn't all that enthusiastic. In the first place, they didn't have anything that cost less than two thousand dollars. And in the second place, he couldn't imagine where an immigrant kid like me was going to get the money anyway. Mr. Clark was the owner of the place. The salesman, who at first was trying to sell me a car, said he didn't have anything in my price range. There was the 150 Series Chevrolet on the low end, the 210 Series in the middle, and the Belaire was at the top of the line with a lot of fancy stuff on it.

Even the Chevrolet 150 series, which was the cheapest available at that time, went for a couple thousand bucks. I had checked around and Chevrolet was the least expensive of the major brands.

Then I discovered they had one 150 model on the lot with 1,500 miles on it. The man told me it was a demonstrator. It had a heater but no radio. It was a dark green two-door, and I liked it. He said, "We'll let you have it for $1,900."

"I don't have $1,900," I replied.

He asked, "How much do you have?"

I told him, "I've got $1,700."

"We cannot let it go for $1,700," he said. But he blinked

and looked at me like he might. He stared at me real hard, squinted his eyes, and asked, "Where is the $1,700?"

"I have it right here," I said, and I pulled out the seventeen crisp one-hundred-dollar bills and counted them out for him.

To say the least, he was stunned. There I was with a map of Lebanon on my face and an accent a mile long. I knew he was wondering, *Where did this kid get that kind of money?*

Anyway, he took me to the sales manager, who asked me, "Can you pay $1,800?"

I said, "All I have is $1,700."

"I'll see if the owner will accept it." So he took me to the owner.

Mr. Clark said to me, "Son, how did you make this money?"

"I sell books and Bibles in the summer," I answered. I asked if he would like to see my Bibles and books. He said he would.

I went out to my bike, and brought in my sample case. I showed him my Bible, and he was genuinely amazed at how beautiful it was and how easy it was to find things in it. Then I showed him the rest of my samples. He was all the more amazed when he realized I had worked eighty-hour weeks all summer, selling these door-to-door, and how I had saved my money.

"How much is that Bible?" he asked.

I told him, "$29.95."

He said, "I would like to buy three of them."

I had never sold anyone three Bibles at once. I was so excited, my hands were trembling.

Then he added, "And I want four Bible storybooks for my grandchildren."

Before I could finish the order for the four Bible storybooks and the three Bibles, he asked the sales manager, "What about you, John?" The salespeople had all been within earshot as I presented the various products to Mr. Clark.

The manager said, "Yeah, I want a Bible and a Bible storybook."

Two or three other salesmen bought a Bible, and some of the secretaries did as well. I was especially pleased to sell so many of these Bibles because a few of them were my demonstrators. Some of them were a little dog-eared; they had some mileage on them. I got rid of all my demonstrators, and I sold about $600 worth of books and Bibles in that Chevrolet dealership!

At the end, Mr. Clark looked me in the eye and said, "This car does not have a radio. Do you like American music?"

I said, "Yes, sir, I love American music. But this car with its little heater is all I can afford. If it didn't get as cold as it does, I'd go without the heater too."

He said, "Okay, I'm going to give you a radio. Will you accept it?"

Tears ran down my cheeks. He put his arm around my shoulders and said, "Son, we are glad to have you here in America. Furthermore, I'm going to give you a brand-new guarantee on this car even though its a demonstrator. If anything goes wrong, this means we will treat it just like a brand-new car. And you tell them Mr. Clark said, 'Fix it!' "

I drove back to the dorm, moved the Bibles and books from my room to the car, and delivered them to my new friends at the dealership.

I walked in with $1,700, and I left with a car and about $300 worth of profit. It was another answer from heaven, a blessing from the Lord. Immediately, I got in my car and drove down to Main Street. I went to the Levy's Department Store. They were having a big 50 percent off sale on clothes and shoes.

For the first time in my life, I bought a Kupenheimer sport coat, a shirt, a tie, and a pair of Florsheim shoes. There I was in my brand-new American coat, shirt, tie, and shoes—and my Chevrolet. I was in "high cotton," and all those clothes cost me less than $100 because of the sale. I went back to school with a brand-new outfit, a brand-new car, my school year paid for in advance, and $200 cash to spare.

That's America!

I was so grateful, so blessed, and so happy. Everybody was thinking, *Oh, Sam, he must have hit the jackpot.* They did not know how hard I worked and the amount of hours and sweat I put out during the summer, the dogs that jumped on me, the doors that were slammed in my face. But that was nothing compared to the joy and rewards I found in what I had been able to achieve.

So during my first summer in Columbia, South Carolina, my love for America grew far greater. And I was beginning to feel much more at home with the American people than when I first arrived.

Before nightfall, I walked back down to the auto agency to pick up my bike.

Chapter Five

A Season of Change

In many respects my second year at Columbia was one of the better years of my life. During that year I learned to depend on God and keep Him central in my life. Students were strongly encouraged to get up early to read the Bible and ask for God's blessing and help for that day. For those who did, this became a great source of blessing. All of this gave me a very positive outlook, and life took on a sense of fullness which had been missing during my first year.

Classes were becoming much easier for me to understand, especially my Bible classes with Prof. Frank Sells and my psychology class with Prof. Buck Hatch. They were both magnificent teachers. Another important class was English, and I greatly profited from my class in history with Dr. George Dollar.

Further, during my second year I was beginning to understand and incorporate more of the American way of life. The standards, expectations, life in general—even the food—began to make more sense. I was beginning to catch on and fit in.

My roommate in the dorm, Jack Hayes, had three years of

French, and that was quite often an enormous help to me. We did this routine where I would say something in French I didn't quite know how to say in English, and he would then translate it for me into English. This way I learned how to express what I was thinking! I could always count on Jack if I needed help.

This was also the year I redeveloped my tendency to be a little rambunctious. Just down the hall in the dorm was Bob Williams. He was a bit mischievous too. One day he knocked on my door. When I opened it, he got me pretty good with a water pistol. I wasn't about to take that without some sort of retaliation.

About an hour and a half later, after he was already in his pajamas and heading to bed, I grabbed a five-gallon mop bucket, filled it with water, and knocked on his door. As he opened the door I threw the whole payload on him. He got soaking wet, of course, but the water also ran right through the wooden floors, the plaster ceiling below, and came down on top of the stationery in the closet of Dean Monroe. A good portion of his office supplies were ruined.

The next morning, to use an Americanism, I was called on the carpet. Dean Monroe confronted me. "Do you see what you have done? You have to pay for this."

Of course he didn't really make me pay for it. The damage wasn't very extensive, but I felt bad enough about the waste. The school was doing the Lord's work, and I had, indeed, been careless in my prank. Anyway, from there on out, Dean Monroe kept an eye on me. I was somewhat mortified because he hardly ever smiled. He was the consummate authoritarian dean. Nevertheless, he was a committed Christian, and I learned to respect his position.

Keeping in Touch

Ever since I arrived in America I had kept my promise to write home faithfully about once a month. But God also made it possible for my father and mother to get special word of my circumstances through an unexpected event.

The Rev. John Haggai came to Columbia to hold a big evangelistic meeting in the fall of 1950 at a city auditorium near the school. There was seating for a couple thousand people, and the place was filled. A bunch of us went from the college to support him as he preached about Christ in this public forum. John Haggai was a handsome, dark-haired man, and, at that time, a pastor in Lancaster, South Carolina.

Since Haggai is a Middle Eastern name, I greeted him after the meeting. "Hi, I'm Sam Ziady."

"Ziady? Where were you born?" he asked.

"I was born in Lebanon," I told him.

John said, "My father came from Syria."

After a year John left Lancaster to pastor a much larger church in Chattanooga, and I saw him again. Later on, after the crowd left, he came back to talk with me, and we got to know each other better. I was wearing my new clothes, and I showed him my brand-new car. I introduced him to some of my managers from the book company.

Shortly thereafter, John Haggai travelled to Lebanon and made it a point to contact my parents. Mama invited him to the house since he was a friend of mine from America. When he arrived, she was preparing lunch. Mama said, "Tell us about Sam."

As Mama put a big feast on the table, John started in.

"What can I tell you about Sam? He has a brand-new car, and he paid for it with cash. Not only that, he has some of the best clothes you have ever seen. And he has money in the bank—it's like he's the banker for the students."

My dad asked, "How did he make that money?"

"Sam's very industrious," John continued. "He's a hard worker, Mr. Ziady. You have to understand he's very smart. You raised him well, and he works very hard."

Mama said, "That's my boy!"

God had made good on my promise that my father would not have to support me in America. He was starting to understand that I had done very well. It was then that my father, almost bursting with pride, said to John, "Well, you know, you can take a sword and put it in a sack of hay, but . . . ."

They didn't have bales of hay in those days. They put the hay in big sacks as tall as a man. From this came a saying that is widely quoted in the Middle East and used by virtually everyone:

> **If you have a sword and you hide it in a hay sack, you can't keep it hidden in there very well. At the slightest pressure the sword will come poking out.**
>
> **Likewise if a man is under pressure, and he has good blood and a strong backbone, he'll show through like the sword and come poking out!**

". . . he's coming out!" my father shouted, completing the saying. "He's coming out! He's more like his grandfather. Sam's got his grandfather's blessing!"

Close Call

Before the school year was over, I had picked up a bunch of the students from CBC in my new Studebaker. I bought this car after I sold my Chevrolet. Everybody piled in to go to Cesa's Diner a few blocks off campus to get a hamburger. It was springtime, and we were full of joy.

On the way I ran straight through a stop sign without even looking. Jimmy Parker, one of my best friends, was in the passenger seat. He saw something enormous out of the corner of his eye and looked to the right. Suddenly, right in front of him, was the face of a huge Greyhound bus bearing down on us like a giant bowling ball. Jimmy thought we were going to get hit and all be killed! He watched in horror as our car escaped impact by what could only have been a couple of inches. Somehow, miraculously, we had gotten by without a scratch. It was time I learned to slow down and be more careful.

A Second Summer, Door-to-Door

When my second school year came to a close, I was very eager to start my summer job again. I would still be selling door-to-door, but I had recruited five other guys to work for me as well. So I was moving into management! We were going to work in Orangeburg, South Carolina, a town about forty-five miles southwest of Columbia.

My team was in Bamberg one day, a smaller town about fifteen miles down the road from Orangeburg. I was on a doorstep presenting a Bible to a woman, and another woman came up to us. She put her finger right on my nose and asked me very directly, "Son, do you know what this Bible talks about?"

I answered, "Yes, ma'am. It talks about God and His Son, Jesus Christ, our Lord and Savior."

She pressed a second question, "Do you have Christ in your life?"

I said, "Yes, ma'am, I certainly do."

She asked another question, "Are you walking the walk?"

I answered, "Yes, ma'am."

She was truly pleased to meet a traveling Bible salesman who was a real Christian. She had become discouraged, hearing about so many salesmen who didn't really believe in the product they sold. Well, we talked for a while, and Mrs. Guy Sanders became a good friend of mine that day. I don't remember if I sold her a Bible or not, but I was so pleased to have made her acquaintance.

Before I left, she invited me to come and spend the nights at her family home when I was in the area. This would save me money on motels and meals. She had three boys, and I think she wanted me to be an influence on one of her sons who was a little younger than I was.

Mr. Sanders even lent me a key to the door! I'd go in and spend the night, and then sometimes I'd have breakfast with the family. He was very glad to be able to help me, and I was very thankful as well. Mr. Sanders owned Sanders Supply and Wholesale Lumber Company in Bamberg. He was the largest lumber dealer around, and they were one of the wealthiest families in town. This whole family reached out to me and truly made me their brother in Christ. Later, when I got married, Mr. and Mrs. Sanders were seated where my parents would have been if they could have been there for the wedding, and their son Guy Jr. was an usher. He and I are still close, and I treasure the memories of the time I spent with this loving family.

Back then my immediate boss was John Dunlap. He was in charge of all the recruiting for South Carolina, among other states, for the International Book Company. He had been a colonel in the army and retired from Fort Jackson. He made a conscious decision to recruit and work with kids selling Bibles and other helpful books door-to-door. Without his guidance, I probably never would have made it as a good salesman and manager.

Maturing

One night it was late, probably around ten o'clock, and I was still out knocking on doors. At one house I suddenly realized I had awakened a gentleman from his bed. He got angry or scared—maybe both—and came up to me and pointed a gun in my face. He evidently thought I was a burglar.

"Sir, I'm not here to steal at all!" I raised my hands and said, "Don't shoot!"

He asked, "What are you here for then?"

I replied, "I'm here to sell you a Bible."

He complained, "Don't you understand it's too late?"

"I wasn't paying any attention to the time," I explained, and apologized. I think he was embarrassed when he heard "Bible."

"Let me see what you're selling!" he said. "What kind of a Bible?"

Reaching for the Bible I said, "If you'll turn your gun away from me I can explain it to you much better!" I showed him the

Bible, being careful to present all the benefits. And sure enough, he bought a Bible that night! I think he felt sorry for frightening me so badly. He became one of my best supporters in the area, and gave me helpful leads and names of prospective customers from that time on.

I made so many friends through the book selling both summers. One of them was Perry Priest, who later went on to mission school, graduated, went out to the field, and became a full-time missionary. He married Dr. McQuilkin's daughter, Ann, and he was one of the guys on my sales team.

What a great summer in Orangeburg. I made more money than the year before, and was all set for the coming year. God was faithfully supplying all that I needed, and more.

What Next?

During the summer of 1952 other important things were happening too. One of my classmates had been pastoring a little Methodist church out in the country. He got married and asked me to substitute for him while he was on his honeymoon. But he had a terrible auto accident, fatally injuring him; his new wife was in a coma for several months.

The impact on the church was devastating, and it was a terrible shock to me as well. But the congregation was wonderful, especially some of the older women. They reached out in Christian charity and comforted me. For instance, they always had a nice supper for me and would give me a big basket of food to take back to campus with me.

Dean Monroe became aware of my association with the Methodists and felt strongly that it was improper. I headed out there on Sundays instead of going to church where I had been a member. He admonished me, "You are a member of the Baptist church. You can't be a Baptist and pastor a Methodist church."

I had been receiving an honorarium of just twenty-five dollars a week, and I had to pay my expenses out of it, so it wasn't as though I was doing it for the money. But the ministry was fruitful and fulfilling. Some of the young people were being brought to Christ, and I think I was a good influence on them. I said, "I'm supposed to do something good in life. I'm helping direct young lives."

Unconvinced, Dean Monroe replied, "You can't do that. You have to resign, leave the school, or join the Methodist church."

I had, for some time, been thinking about what I should do with my life and whether or not to stay at Columbia. So I started to set some goals. First, I wanted to take more business courses. Second, I wanted to get a degree from an accredited college, and CBC wasn't accredited at that time. Third, I wanted to widen my educational horizon. Later, I discovered that after two years, I could not transfer much of my coursework at CBC to an accredited school. This came as an unpleasant surprise.

The dean of arts and sciences at the nearby University of South Carolina (USC), Dr. Francis Bradley, was a wonderful human being. He extended to me the hand of fellowship and support when I went to talk with him about transferring. He also enjoyed conversing with me in French, and we developed quite a friendship. He tested me on my French and discovered I was quite proficient.

He hit upon the idea of awarding me credit for passing

equivalency exams in courses of study in which I was already fairly advanced. He told me if I would take and pass French 31 and 32, they would give me credit for all the prerequisites: French 11, 12, 21, and 22. This was incredibly helpful. The same thing happened in accounting and economics—I received six credits each. I made up the remaining credits by taking additional courses offered at USC, and was able to graduate in two years. And, thanks to Dean Bradley's advocacy, I enrolled at resident tuition rates—saving me a bundle. I have nothing but a warm spot in my heart for this dear man who was always there to help me.

An Official Name Change

In 1952, one of the district attorneys in the State of South Carolina was Pugh Taylor. His wife was a beautiful Christian, and they had a home on several hundred acres, almost across from the little Methodist church I pastored. Occasionally, Mrs. Taylor would come to the church on Sunday. She got to know me and invited me to their beautiful white house for dinner. She thought I would be a good influence on her boys.

One evening Mr. Taylor and I got to talking. He enjoyed hearing stories about the old country, and I was fascinated with his experiences too. We became good friends, and I made it a point to stay in touch. After I graduated from USC he became a judge and also a Sunday school teacher at a big church downtown.

I had been living in the U.S. for several years, and I had gotten special permission to work so I could pay my tuition. By 1954 I was seriously thinking of becoming an American citizen.

I was finally notified that I would be issued a green card, an official work permit, and I had to appear in Judge Pugh Taylor's court.

When my day in court arrived, I realized this was the first time I had ever been in an American courtroom. I had no idea what a judge did or what to expect. A nervous feeling came over me, as if I were walking into the presence of God or something. The bailiff came in shouting, "Stand ye, stand ye!" And BANG, the gavel came down. He shouted again, "The judge is coming, the judge is coming."

I stood up as Judge Taylor entered the courtroom.

Then the bailiff commanded us, "Sit ye down, sit ye down. The judge is here."

The judge was a big man as it was, and wearing that black robe, sitting so high up at his bench, he was quite an imposing figure. There were three or four of us there for immigration matters. In college everyone called me Sam rather than my given name, Salim. But I had always used my last name Ziady. He finally said, "Mr. Ziady."

I stood and answered, "Yes, Your Honor."

He began immediately with the ceremony. "Do you pledge to uphold the laws of the United States of America?"

I answered, "Yes, sir."

He asked me directly, "Do you want to live and work in America?"

I answered, "Yes, sir."

He said, "Your name is Ziady. Is that the name you would like to retain as a registered alien?"

I explained to him that the meaning of *Ziady* is "more" or it could also be in English something like "extra," or "plus."

He smiled at me as if to say, "That's nice." Then he suggested, "While in Rome, do as the Romans do. What do you want to be?" He was insinuating that eventually I'd be happier with a more American-sounding last name, but I had never really thought that through. He put the ball in my court.

I felt paralyzed. I began shaking. Why was I so scared in front of this friend who is a judge? Finally, he slammed the gavel down and said, "In Rome we do as the Romans do."

So I came in "Ziady"; I went out "Moore."

The name should have actually been "More," but the court reporter made a mistake. She spelled it M-o-o-r-e. I knew on the spot it wasn't correct. But it would have been such a headache to raise my hand and reopen the process that I just left it.

Dealing with Disappointment

After I graduated from the University of South Carolina in the spring of 1954, I still wasn't sure what God had planned for me. So I decided to come back for graduate school. I took graduate courses at USC, plus some graduate work at Columbia Seminary, twelve credit hours at each school. I had the money, so I was very glad to be able to have the opportunity to buckle down and pursue the two graduate degrees simultaneously.

My thesis at Columbia was to be on the history of education in the Middle East and the difference between the French system and the English system. During one course the teacher asked if I was going to the mission field. I told her I wasn't sure what God wanted me to do. She became very upset with me, because she felt I ought to go back and serve my people in

Lebanon. It was very awkward. Soon she became outraged, suggesting I had "come to school under false pretenses."

I finally snapped back and told her, "I think my serving God is between me and Him, not between you and God."

She was able to use her influence to see to it that my thesis was never accepted. Without any explanation, my thesis was turned down flat after I had finished all my classes for a master's degree. I was told I would have to completely rewrite the paper. We were at an impasse. Several people who had read it were impressed with the research I had done.

This was very rough on me. Honestly, it tore me up on the inside. It seemed unfair that I could be penalized in such an arbitrary and manipulative way. After all this time, it was my first bad experience in America. I did not let this episode turn me sour toward Columbia Bible College. Though I felt I got a raw deal, I could not really resolve anything. The school was going through major changes. Dr. McQuilkin, in poor health, entered Duke University Medical Hospital. He had passed away in 1952, and an interim president was appointed shortly thereafter.

The apostle Paul says, "In everything give thanks" (1 Thess. 5:18 NKJV), and I decided to do exactly that. I felt the education I received was more important than the degree anyway, and when I let go of this issue, it let go of me.

About fifteen years later my old classmate, Bob Yount, called to invite me to attend the alumni association get-together, and I revealed to him that I wasn't actually a graduate. I related how I had completed all the coursework and explained why I never was awarded my degree. He was very disappointed, and he told the whole story to the current president, Dr. Robertson

McQuilkin, son of the founder and my legal guardian. A few months later Dr. McQuilkin came to Nashville and personally handed me my master's degree certificate.

Finding Myself

As a result of recruiting interviews on the campus of the University of South Carolina, I had several opportunities I could pursue. One was with IBM, another with GE, and one with the Chase Manhattan Bank.

Lots of thoughts were running through my mind. What did I want to do? I thought I would like to become an international banker. So I went to New York to work for "The Chase." I loved the big city. It had such challenge and appeal for a single guy like me. However, there was a problem. I wasn't earning enough money to live on.

Shortly after I arrived in the Big Apple, my boss became a vice president. At a special party they held in his honor, I asked him, "How long have you been with the bank?"

"Fourteen years," he answered.

You could have knocked me over with a feather. I was hoping to become vice president within two years, running my own bank, maybe in Casablanca. Or, if I were lucky, in Paris or some other exotic place. Devastated, I realized that a job with The Chase is not the fast track. I began making plans to get out of there. To sort things out I took a leave of absence and went back to Lebanon to see my father and mother. It had been six years. I missed them and all the old familiar places. I stayed for about a month.

My father was very proud of me; I had graduated, I made

good grades, and I didn't have to ask him for any money. He knew I had money in the bank. "No doubt you are going to go back to America, aren't you?" he asked.

"Yes," I replied.

He asked, "Are you going to live permanently in America?"

"Maybe," I told him. "I want to live in America for a while longer to see if I like it."

The conversation paused for a bit. Then I said, "People in America don't understand how good they have it. And above all, they don't appreciate the freedom they have. Dad, you can drive from New York to California without hardly stopping. This is the kind of freedom I have there. Besides that, any American can choose any profession, work as long as he wants, and make what he wants."

Freedom is what has kept me in America. I have come to believe that feeling free is a sensation only an immigrant from the Old World can really understand. I was a young man from that Old World, extremely conscious of the freedom to choose, the freedom to work, the freedom to worship.

That went a long way with me. But my father didn't seem to think it was all that important.

Father's Advice

As Dad reluctantly drove me back to the airport, we continued to talk about my future.

I told him that even while I was a double graduate student, I made $13,200 selling books. I had about forty to fifty students working for me. Now I was working for the Chase Bank and making only $7,800. I had what amounted to two college degrees, I spoke several languages. I was single and in good health, and I began to think I was being too conservative. Dad couldn't understand why I would work at the bank.

I tried to explain it to him. "First you have to learn the banking business and even with a lower salary, at least there is security for me," I said.

His eyes popped open wide, and he yelled, "Security? A man like you? What kind of security do you want? With two college degrees and three languages, what other security do you need to have?"

His response caught me off guard.

He went on, "I thought your faith in God was the greatest security you have. You keep talking about faith and hope. What is this faith? If you have faith in God, you should have faith in yourself."

What could I say?

"Son, listen to me. Let me give you some advice. Be honest, work hard, and don't be afraid to take a chance." That tripod formula for success has never left me.

When I landed in New York I was so glad to get back I got down on my hands and knees and kissed the ground! My dad was right. I had fallen in love with America, and I wanted to live here. But I still wasn't sure what God wanted me to do.

Chapter Six

A Turning Point

When I got home to America in 1957, I went down to Nashville to see my brother Chuck and show him the pictures I had taken of our parents and the old country. He had migrated to America in 1955, and was a junior at Vanderbilt University. We were having a good visit, and we got to talking about the future. By this time, he had sold books for me over two summers.

He said to me, "Sam, you're too good. You should start your own business."

I countered, "I don't have that much capital. More people fail in business because of lack of capital than anything else."

He came back to it again. "You could start small and grow the business."

I wasn't sure I wanted to start my own business. I had been thinking of a move to Atlanta. I have always loved that city and had an offer pending with General Electric there. GE's reputation for giving young managers excellent job training was second to none. The company is especially helpful in teaching people how to analyze business problems, understand balance sheets, and deal effectively with cash flow situations and return on assets. My plan had been to recruit a few kids in Nashville that summer, make some good money, then move to Atlanta and work for GE.

The National Book Company

But largely due to Chuck's encouragement—and my father's advice—I decided I would take a chance and start up my own company. I called it the National Book Company. The John A. Hertel Company, a Bible and reference book publisher in Chicago, allowed me to buy their books wholesale if I agreed not to compete for two years in North and South Carolina or Georgia.

"No problem, I can work in Tennessee," I told them. I recruited about twenty kids in the Nashville area from Middle Tennessee State, Freewill Baptist Bible College, Vanderbilt, and Scarritt. I worked hard with them, and I made about $27,000 for the summer—over three times what I was making at The Chase in an entire year! And the bank had paid me $1,000 more than an MBA from Harvard would earn. So book sales was a much better opportunity for me, no matter how I looked at it.

But I wasn't entirely comfortable being in the door-to-door book business. It was grueling work for one thing, and there was no alternative to the traveling the job required. At summer's end I still was tempted to close the book operation and go to Atlanta. But three or four of the kids who had done well came to me and said, "Look, Mr. Moore, if you close down and don't let us sell next summer, we won't be able to go back to school."

If anyone could appreciate their situation it was I. I knew exactly how they felt. So I finally decided to take a job during the winter working for the Provident Bond Plan Company so I could work with the student sales teams again during the next year's summer months.

Provident sold bonds to nonprofit organizations, such as churches and schools, to help them raise money for building and other capital expenditures. A church could empower Provident to sell bonds to its members. The church would get the money it needed as soon as Provident had bonds out to the members of the congregation covering the amount the church needed to borrow. This was really a loan from the members to the congregation.

The church would, in turn, pay back the bond to the bondholders with interest at just a little less than a bank would charge for large mortgage loans. It was a win-win arrangement, with the church getting the cash at a better interest rate and the parishioners earning a decent return on their loan while helping their church and the community.

Providentially (pun intended), one of the churches I worked with was Princeton Presbyterian Church in Johnson City, Tennessee, a wonderful city in the eastern part of the state near the Virginia border. The church wanted to issue a bond program and raise $175,000 in the fall of 1957. Church leaders came to me with a reference from Mrs. Janelle Bowman, a fine Christian lady who raised six children and sent some of them to Columbia Bible College. She ran a jewelry store in Johnson City.

I made a presentation to the church and they accepted my proposal. As I recall, I had to prepare the paperwork to incorporate that church. This involved writing a set of bylaws. Then I charted a schedule of payments and came up with a plan that would, over a period of thirteen years, redeem the bonds with interest from the church through the First People's Bank in Johnson City.

Dear Peggy

It was while I was working and living in Johnson City in 1957 that I met Peggy Poe. She worked for the Social Security Administration, and was a member of Princeton Presbyterian Church.

In the evening she would come to the church and do the typing for the bond program and help keep track of the records. I was often there at the same time, putting the proposal together for their bond sales program. We usually finished up about the same time, so we would shut the lights off and lock up together. We began going out for ice cream or coffee afterward.

I first noticed Peggy on an earlier occasion at the church. She was playing the organ, and I figured she probably was already married. The church that evening was full. When she finished playing, she came down to sit with the congregation, and there was no place for her but right next to me in the front row. I looked down and saw she was not wearing a ring.

It wasn't long before we both realized we liked each other. Then I began to fall in love with Peggy. Without her, I discovered, I felt rather lonesome. She was steady and easygoing. I was twenty-seven years old and she was twenty-two. She, too, was in love with me.

I had by now decided I wanted to stay in America, and I

felt Peggy would make a great wife. I was careful not to tell her until I firmly made up my mind about marrying her. I didn't want to lead her on. Little did I realize how soon I would make that decision! It couldn't have been more than about four months after we met that I asked her to marry me.

I bought a nice ring for Peggy from Beckner's jewelry store. Like the lady on the doorstep years before, Mrs. Bowman stuck her finger at my nose. "If you mislead this girl I will kill you! She comes from a wonderful home, her father is dead, and she is the main support for her mother." Peggy was an only child. Her mother, at the time, was not old enough to receive widow's Social Security benefits.

I told her, "Don't worry, Mrs. Bowman. Anyone I commit to marry, I am going to take good care of." So I bought the ring for Peggy. After less than a year of engagement, we were married on October 25, 1958, which happens to be my birthday. It was my second year in the book business in Nashville.

I was initially attracted to Peggy because she was beautiful—tall, fair complected, and slender. But I later discovered that she also had a very sweet Christian spirit. She was easygoing with a lovely temperament.

By contrast, I've always been a tornado—a fast-lane fireball. I knew she would be a perfect match for me as I anticipated the pressure I would face in the business world. What a sweet, agreeable, and pleasant personality she has. I thank God that this match was made in heaven. Marrying Peggy is the best decision I've ever made and the greatest blessing God has ever sent into my life.

In 1961, we still had an apartment in Johnson City where Peggy was working. I was commuting back and forth to

Nashville. We were, for all intents and purposes, living on the money she made. Whatever I made, we put back into the business. Once you start financing your own receivables it takes all the cash you can put into it, especially if you are growing.

Back to the Books

I decided to stay with the name "National Book Company," and we commenced business under a special arrangement with International Book Company. We would sell a Bible for $34.95, at which point the customer paid us $4.95 down on the total purchase price. International Book Company handled it from there with their credit department. They paid me the rest of the money, less a reserve for bad debt and collection expenses.

It worked out well for the first couple of years or so. But later on I found out they kept on record the names of my customers and the salesmen who made each sale. One of my best sales managers was in Memphis. We had established a small office there and had several salesmen working out of that location. We were selling five or six thousand Bibles a year out of Memphis.

But that sales manager decided he wanted to leave and be in business for himself. So he went to the owner of the International Book Company, which owned the John A. Hertel Company, and arranged to buy the same books they had been selling me at the same wholesale price. I had set him up, helped train him, and financed the office.

It didn't set well at all with me. Then and there I decided to go into Bible publishing for myself.

Chapter Seven

A Series of Setbacks

Jack Clay was my banker at Third National Bank. The president there was Sam Fleming, a very influential man in Nashville. I enjoyed doing business there, and Jack was a good banker—an honest man whom I had learned to trust. In fact, it was through Jack that I borrowed my first $1,000, and during the next five start-up years over $200,000 more. Frequently I needed more capital. Mr. Clay eventually suggested that National Book Company, go public, and he introduced me to the J. C. Bradford Company and to Equitable Securities.

I had been thinking about publishing for some time, and I knew exactly what I would publish if I got the chance. I wanted to produce the best Bible the world had ever seen. It would contain beautiful four-color photographs of the Holy Land and of classic religious art, and there would be study helps for the average reader so it could be understood by anyone without having to learn an outdated dialect of the English language first. I had already been investing time and resources into this project and had some excellent tools in development.

I decided to take my new publishing company public under the name Royal Publishers. Mr. Owen of Equitable recommended to me Mr. Nathan McCauley from Asheville, North Carolina, who was a member of the New York Stock Exchange since Equitable did not handle any underwriting under a million, and I was trying to raise $300,000. He had an office in Asheville, as well as several other offices in North Carolina and East Tennessee. Mr. Owen contacted him and arranged for us to speak each other on the phone and to get acquainted. Mr. McCauley was willing and able to take us public. He asked me to have an independent audit, have the statements certified, and then file the forms to go public under the name Royal Publishers.

Mr. McCauley felt it would be best to put the National Book Company and the little finance company I had started called National Honor Plan together under the umbrella of the new company. We merged National Book and National Honor Plan into Royal Publishers, and I agreed to take stock in Royal Publishers. The net worth of the company at that time was about $150,000, excluding all the planning and development costs for the Bible index we'd been working on, the clarification notes, and various other helps.

We planned to sell $300,000 in stock. I intended to own half of the company while the investors would own the other half. This stock offering would sufficiently capitalize the new business.

A Case of Blue Monday

However, the day we were supposed to go public was the day the financial world remembers as Blue Monday, May 1962. The market crashed.

Shares of IBM and GE and other major companies plummeted by almost 50 percent in one day! The crash was precipitated by the business community's loss of confidence in the federal government. There were many who feared the Kennedy administration's objectives and goals. The specific event that triggered this plunge involved a conflict between Roger Blough, chairman of US Steel, and Attorney General Robert Kennedy. On the night before the crash, I understood that Blough was handcuffed and taken away for interrogation for increasing the price of steel at his company, and for standing up to the president.

The Kennedy administration wanted to stabilize the price of steel, a crucial commodity in the U.S. economy. They were serious enough about it to apply pressure through many avenues, all the while warning the entire business community not to increase prices. This sent bad signals to the steel industry and to the entire world of business, and the market headed south at the opening. It was a disaster.

Mr. McCauley rightly decided this was not the time for us to go public. We had already incorporated the company, sent the files and papers to the SEC for approval, done all the legal work, and completed the audit. It was an awful feeling, and it left me between a rock and a hard place. I decided I had to try to find a way to go forward in spite of the collapse. With the stock market in utter disarray, we still needed capital, badly. It seemed as if the whole world had caved in on me, and I was trapped.

I prayed.

Then I went to see my banker, Mr. Clay, again. He recommended I find five or six private investors. "But keep it a small group," he told me, "so you can hold better control of the company." But with the market still in bad shape, he thought I should wait.

I told him, "I've spent too much time and money to stop now. Is there someone else who could take us public?"

"There's a small company here named Tennessee Securities," he said. "But I don't know whether they'd be willing to do it in the environment we're in. Besides, they are new and not well known."

The business atmosphere was bad, they warned me, but Tennessee Securities said they were willing to give it their best shot. So we teamed up with them to make the offering. We were listed over the counter (OTC). It took them two or three months, but Tennessee Securities sold the stock and we raised $300,000 from the public before the end of 1962.

One of the shareholders, by the way, was Mrs. Morrow Graham, Billy Graham's mother, whom I had met a decade earlier. She bought one hundred shares of stock and said to me, "My boy, I'm so proud of you that you're going to publish Bibles. I'll be praying for you every day. I know you are going to do a good job."

I was very touched. "Mother Graham, thank you. God bless you. And I do need your prayers!"

Another person who invested was my old college friend Elmer Towns. He and his wife had invested in United, American, and Delta Airlines through their credit union as a kind of retirement fund. I told them, "Sell it and put it all in Royal Publishers. I guarantee you, if you lose any money, I'll make it up to you. But you'll make money." Elmer saw that small amount grow tremendously over the next several years.

Mr. Carl Young, president of the Giant Grocery Company in Johnson City, became chairman of our board. Besides his initial purchase, toward the end of the offering he bought additional stock in the company. He believed in me and treated me as if he were my father.

Growing up in North Carolina, Carl moved to East Tennessee and started a small wholesale grocery company, which grew to become Giant Foods. He was respected throughout the region, and very successful. This man, an elder at First Presbyterian Church in Johnson City, became my sounding board, a great adviser, and a great confidant. I, in return, loved him and would have walked through fire for him. We had a great chemistry, love, and respect between us.

That first year Royal Publishers did about $120,000 worth of business. Like my father before me, I had started again, from scratch. Blue Monday had been overcome.

Wanting a Family

Our second setback was far more personal. Peggy and I had been married nearly three years and had tried to begin our family, but to no avail. Peggy was beginning to feel brokenhearted. Her physician was Dr. Lawrence E. Gordon in Johnson City. His roommate back in medical school happened to be Roy Parker, now the head of the gynecology department at Duke

University Medical School. He had helped deliver some of the Eisenhower and Nixon children. I was sure he was not about to see a simple book peddler from East Tennessee.

His old roommate, Dr. Gordon, called him. "Look, this is an important situation. Please try to see them."

He made an appointment for us with Dr. Parker on May 18, 1961. We drove all the way to Durham, North Carolina, to meet him at the diagnostic clinic at Duke. We both went through a series of outpatient tests. My tests came back first. Dr. Parker said, "Sam, you're okay."

After Peggy's tests came back, Dr. Parker gently advised her, "You've got some trouble." But he explained that she could undergo corrective surgery and there would still be only a fifty-fifty chance we could have a baby. She did not hesitate and jumped at the opportunity. She was ready then and there to have the operation.

I cautioned her, "No, you have to think about it first, honey. I didn't marry you for babies, I married you to love you and live with you. If God gives us babies that will be His blessing. We should not interfere."

She countered, "But God leads us to doctors, and works His miracles through them. If they can help us—"

I interrupted her. "Let's think about it for a few days."

We returned to Johnson City, and after a week passed Peggy still insisted on the surgery. We called and scheduled the operation. In the meantime we continued to pray about the outcome of the surgery. In August 1961 Peggy had the corrective surgery, performed by Dr. Roy Parker at Duke University Medical School Hospital.

In six months a baby was conceived! On the evening of

November 2, 1962, I took Peggy to the hospital. As I was sitting in the waiting room, the guy next to me, who already had two girls, got the news he was a father again—another girl. The guy on the other side of me, who also had a girl, received the report that his wife had just had another girl.

I smiled nervously at both of them, and then I got up and walked out. "Lord, this is 'Girls Night'! What am I doing here!" Both Peggy and I had wanted to start out with a boy. That was part of the culture I'd grown up in, and it meant a lot to us.

Suddenly, Dr. Charles Hillman, a partner of Dr. Gordon's, came out of the delivery room carrying a blanket-wrapped baby. He found me in the hall and announced, "Sam, this is your baby. This is your baby boy!"

"Let me see, Doctor!" I said.

I looked and saw that big baby boy. I remember looking at his spindly legs. Then I said, "God, I can't believe it." I started jumping up and down, thanking God he was healthy and that he was a boy. Peggy was already asleep, so they cleaned the baby up and put him down to sleep as well.

Driving back to the house that night, I began to think about how God had given us a son. It was a special blessing to us because in the old country, as I have noted, a first-born son was a symbol of God's goodness. It meant the continuation of the family name, influence, and prosperity. I understand how in this day and age it may sound inappropriate to some. But if life in America teaches us anything, it teaches us respect for the diversity of our cultures and traditions. So this was a guilt-free celebration for me! And a very special gift from the God of my fathers.

Let me also say that no father in all history has loved his

daughters more than I have loved mine! They know it, and I know it. All children are miraculous and special gifts from God, and I treasure mine beyond compare. But the gift of a son being our firstborn was exquisite, and I couldn't wait to call home to Lebanon and break the news to my father.

"Dad, we had a baby."

He said, "Yes? Is it a—"

"It's very healthy," I broke in, stringing him along.

"Good," Dad said. "Is it a b—?"

"Weighs nearly ten pounds," I teased, interrupting him again.

"But what is it?" he demanded, by now growing impatient and somewhat annoyed.

I couldn't hold back my joy any longer, and I finally shouted, "Dad, it's a boy!"

Then he started screaming. "Thank God, it's a boy. Mama, it's a boy!"

I blinked back the tears.

Then he asked, "How is Peggy?"

I said, "Everything is good." And it was good, so wonderful and precious.

He told me later that after I hung up, he got out his pistol and started firing up toward the sky until he emptied the clip— a Lebanese custom of great celebration. He stood on the porch and shot again and again until all the bullets had been fired—a salute into the air for his new grandson, the son of his eldest son. Great joy and a deep sense of the fulfillment of God's promise permeated our home.

Peggy and I decided to name him Samuel Joseph. In the Bible it says, "It came to pass in the process of time that Hannah conceived and bore a son, and called his name Samuel, saying, 'Because I have asked for him from the LORD' " (1 Sam. 1:20 NKJV). *Joseph* means "increaser," and the story of Joseph in Genesis is one of our favorite family Bible stories. Now, against the odds, we were a family.

In the face of barrenness, God had overcome adversity for us.

Learning the Trade

Peggy and I decided I should open an office in Johnson City and operate out of there since most of my directors were from East Tennessee. Earl Reazor was the president of People's Bank; Welsford Arts was a member of the Hamilton National Bank Board of Directors and the largest real estate broker in the area; Carl Jones was the publisher of the Johnson City *Press-Chronicle* and owner of the radio station. Nearby was Ben Haden, editor and publisher of the Kingsport, Tennessee, paper; Kyle M. Hart was the former president and chairman of the board of National Savings Corporation, a life insurance holding company in Murfreesboro; and W. T. Crockett Jr. from Nashville was the president of W. T. Crockett & Co., a large manufacturer of water heaters.

Ruby Schum was my personal secretary at Royal Publishers. Her husband was the Rev. Henry Schum, and he was the minister who married Peggy and me at the Princeton Presbyterian Church.

In these early years, I honestly didn't know much about publishing. I was a salesman and a motivator. Nevertheless, we had raised the money, and I felt we were ready to proceed. It was important to commence business as soon as we could, because preliminary planning and preparation had already consumed the first two years of our operation.

But how was I ever going to learn what I needed to know about publishing? There weren't any books or courses of study that explained how to print a Bible!

The more I thought about it, I realized one of the biggest book manufacturing plants in the world was right in my own backyard. I decided to start going over to Kingsport Press, located about fifteen miles from where I was living, in the evenings. I would watch the printers, see how they changed plates, and learn how they printed encyclopedias and other books. I discovered how they worked the color presses, how they used web presses, and when they would use sheet-fed presses. They taught me about different paper stocks and explained the components needed for a quality book-manufacturing operation.

I remember one night the roll of paper broke. It was a mess: paper everywhere, loud warning sirens in the plant and total chaos. But in less than a half hour, the crew had rethreaded the web and gotten everything back on-line. I later found out that the customer had decided to run a less expensive paper, and this was only one of numerous breaks that had occurred during the run. Even in the world of book production, cheaper isn't always better.

I asked a lot of questions, and most of the guys were very helpful and patient with me. I think they could tell I had a passion, and they were glad to lend me a hand. It was the very best sort of hands-on Bible manufacturing education I could have possibly received.

My dream almost from the time I arrived in America was to

publish a better, more useful Bible than anyone had ever produced before. My focus was this: People would buy a great Bible if they knew where to get one. I wanted to create a beautifully bound, family-type Bible with a special index, a concordance, a dictionary, and introductions to the Old and New Testaments as well as to each book. I would include color pictures of the Holy Land and of religious art, and additional unique study helps that would assist the average Christian in personally understanding the Bible. Although this was a complete departure from the many other Bibles published in America, I was confident people would buy it if I could produce what I saw in my mind's eye.

But another setback was in the wings.

A Brush with Disaster

In producing the Bible I wanted to use the best color illustrations available. In my personal possession were scores of beautiful color transparencies, photos I had collected of the Holy Land. These pictures would bring new clarity to the study of Old and New Testament geography.

Further, I wanted to include the Christian renderings of Rembrandt, Rubens, Van Dyck, and all of the great classical artists. I visited museums and art houses all across the country that held the rights for these paintings. We finally selected five hundred pictures and then narrowed them down to about two hundred. We cropped them and marked them so they would be ready for color separation.

Jim Sams at Kingsport Press and Joe Maliccot was the head of his own printing company in Bristol, Tennessee. Both were dedicated Christians and great friends. For many evenings we looked at each transparency through a device that allowed us to magnify the illustration to the actual size we wanted to print on paper. Each night when we finished, I would put those transparencies back into a large brown envelope nearly two inches thick and drive home with them. I'd always keep them in the house.

One night I said to myself, *I'm not going to bring them into the house. I'll just slide them under the seat of the car so they're here when we meet tomorrow night.* That night I left them in the car, the first and only time I ever did so.

That same night, at 2:30 in the morning on July 4, 1963, I heard a loud knock on our bedroom window. I got out of bed, a little groggy, and looked for my robe. Peggy was sound asleep. Was someone trying to break in? The guy kept on knocking, and I could hear him urging, "Hurry, hurry—get up!"

I opened our bedroom window and called out, "What's the matter with you? What do you want?"

He said, "Your house is on fire."

I said, "One second."

I opened our bedroom door into the living room and saw that the curtains were engulfed in flames. I couldn't make out much of anything for the smoke. Joe's room, like ours, adjoined the living room. I looked over at his door and it was almost completely shut. Usually we left it open. I knew instantly that if the door to his room had been open, little Samuel Joseph, nine months old, would probably have died of smoke inhalation.

I rushed in and grabbed my son, wrapped him up, and slammed the door shut to the living room. I ran over and opened his bedroom window and gave him to the man outside.

When I returned to our room to rouse Peggy, she was up and had already called the fire department.

Our rescuer worked nights at Colonial Bakery, and he got off work at 2:30 every morning. He saw the fire as he drove by the house and stopped to help. The fire department arrived on the scene and knocked out the blaze, but we had extensive fire, smoke, and water damage.

Somehow, in God's mercy, not only were we saved as a family, but we had the pictures! They would have been ruined if I had brought them into the house. Our son was safe, and the Bible project was secure. The next morning I got on my knees and said, "God, I don't know why, but it's a miracle that You saved my son and the pictures together." We nearly lost the house, but my family was safe. Our insurance would pay for most of the repairs.

Still another setback would be overcome.

Chapter Eight

Our First Bible

The man in charge of reconstructing my house told me it would be at least a month, maybe two, before we could move back in. So after a couple of days in a motel, I said to Peggy, "Let's go to the old country!" She smiled and nodded in agreement. This lifted her spirits and proved to be just the thing she needed to take her mind off the house. She was also eager to see my homeland and meet my relatives for the first time. For my part, I was eager to show my son to his grandfather, grandmother, and the rest of the family.

Before we left, I packed a small camera, an Argus C-3 with an extra lens. I would be able to take additional photos in the Holy Land for use in the Bible. When we got to Beirut I purchased another camera, especially suited for taking professional-grade outdoor photographs. This Bible was marked for excellence!

The visit was epic in its meaning for us as a family. We had returned to Lebanon full of hope and grateful for all God's loving-kindness in our lives.

On our second day there we visited with my grandmother. It was then she told me that before her husband, my grandpa Kahlil, died he had made her promise to give the blessing of the Lord to my son if he was gone when that day came. With tears, Peggy and I watched as she prayed and blessed Joe out on the balcony, that he would be made to prosper spiritually and physically in the name of the Lord. What a remarkable time this was for us.

A few days later, I drove up into the Cedars of Lebanon to take pictures of the mountains and the beautiful trees. The photos turned out extremely well. So well, in fact, that I decided to drive down to Palestine. I wanted to get some additional shots of the Holy Land, perhaps enough for future Bible projects as well. My father, my brother Mike, and I drove to Amman, Jordan, and then over into Jerusalem.

We were able to get pictures of the tomb of Christ at Golgotha, various views of Bethlehem, the Mount of Olives, Rachel's tomb, the Sea of Galilee, and many other historic sights. I was so fortunate in having success with some of the photos I took that when our first Bible was published these photos won an award in *Moody Monthly* magazine in the Bible category: Pictures of the Year, 1965.

The pictures alone were worth more than ten times what the trip cost me. What a way to wait for a house to be repaired from a fire! Once again, it was like hitting two birds with one stone.

The Team and the Tasks

Back when we organized Royal Publishers, I began looking for a team of Bible scholars, people who could contribute the unique features I wanted to include in our first Bible. Some would be old acquaintances, many others would be new to me. The excitement I felt is difficult for me to describe. I began to expect that this was going to work!

I had attended a men's retreat in Montreat, North Carolina, where Dr. Manford Gutzke was one of the speakers. He knew the language of the Bible so well and had such a marvelous gift for teaching it. He made it possible—even easy—for average people to understand a passage, be moved by it, and be changed.

When I got back I told my secretary, Ruby, about him. It turned out that her husband had studied under Dr. Gutzke, and they thought very highly of him. We all agreed he was a gifted scholar and a superb communicator. He had never written anything for publication. I had no clear notion of how to approach him with my hopes and dreams. How should I propose my idea about including his insights and knowledge of Hebrew and Greek in my new Bible?

Somehow, I arranged a meeting with him. Before I left, Ruby and I and several of the people in the office got together to ask God to go with me and give me wisdom as I spoke about all this with Dr. Gutzke. I decided to take a wide-margin Oxford Bible with me, and I met him and his wife at their home in Decatur, Georgia.

Mrs. Gutzke was a petite woman with wonderful spirit. As I spoke with her husband, I told him what a great scholar I felt he was and how much he had helped me in Montreat. Then I asked him the big question: Did he have any of his text clarifications written down? Had he ever thought of recording these word-by-word explanations?

"No," he said, "I just do it as I teach." He had not put any of it down on paper.

I said, "You know, Dr. Gutzke, you are a man who is already more than sixty years old. When you die all of that knowledge you have is going to go with you. That would be a terrible waste. It would be wonderful if we could get it in print so even more people could benefit from your insights."

"How do you propose I do that? I hardly have time to teach as it is. I'm pulled from all directions," he countered.

I told him, "I have an idea. I have a Bible here with a wide margin, and no doubt you read the Bible on a daily basis?"

"Yes," he answered.

I said, "All you have to do is write down in your own handwriting the meaning of difficult words as you read each day. Use everyday English. Make it easy for the average layman to understand the verse. This is how we can preserve your knowledge. We will print your work in a center-column reference as a translation—your translation—and we'll give you credit for it."

Then Mrs. Gutzke said, "Why, that sounds like a good idea, Manford." I knew the Lord was on my side when Mrs. Gutzke said that.

"No," he said, "that will be too much trouble."

For me that meant go on! Counting on God while trying to be persuasive, I encouraged him, "All you have to do is try. Try it for a month and see how it works out."

He asked for $5,000. I told him we would give him twice that much. That made him even happier. He took the project on a trial basis, and he sent me a sample of the book of Genesis within a couple of weeks. When I received it, I was ecstatic. I called him and told him it was fantastic. I asked Ruby Schum and Loretta Lawson to help us type his material, check the spelling, and arrange his definitions in the right order for the manuscript.

Manford George Gutzke turned out to be one of my core team members. I had great faith in him. He was a professor of Bible at Columbia Theological Seminary in Decatur, the official Presbyterian seminary for the southern states region. Dr. Gutzke, who was of Jewish background, had converted to Christ as a young man and was a great believer. Few knew the Bible as well as he did, and his command of biblical Hebrew was second to none. I am so grateful to God for bringing us together.

For the New Testament, Dr. Gutzke was assisted by Dr. Roy Helton. He held a Ph.D. and was a professor at Belmont College in Nashville, Tennessee. He assisted in proofreading and special editing for Dr. Gutzke, and general editorial work for the New Testament.

Dr. Wick Broomall, who had been my professor of apologetics at Columbia, became the architect of the specialized index I wanted to include. I later learned he had already been working on a similar project. He was an accomplished scholar who had earned his doctorate from Princeton Theological Seminary. Moreover, he was a godly man. Again, I can hardly express the thrill I felt when he agreed to revise his work on the index and do a new one.

The cyclopedic index he produced is a cross between a

concordance and a dictionary, combining the benefits of both. With it, the pastor or layman can find in alphabetical order all the major subject references in the Bible, about ten thousand entries. Back then, there was little along these lines for the average person who wanted to study the Bible.

Other scholars, such as Don Hoke, Wayne Ward, Duke McCall, Samuel Schultz, Everett Harrison, George Ladd, Homer Kent, Robert Mounce, Alfred Martin, David Hubbard, Wilbur Smith, Porter Barrington, Merril Unger, and many more wrote the introductions to the books of the Bible, and other study helps.

Their work was so thorough, Pat Zondervan, head of the company bearing his name, persuaded me to do an edition that he could distribute from Grand Rapids. We produced a special edition for the Zondervan Publishing House of the large family Bible that we sold door-to-door. It included a few additional features that made it different from ours. Pat found immediate acceptance of this new Bible in the Christian book stores. It did so well that I eventually realized we needed to capitalize on this burgeoning bookstore market ourselves. Several years later this led us to hire Bernard Deeter and develop our own Christian trade bookstore presence. No longer would Royal products simply be sold door-to-door.

Success at Last!

In 1964 we published our first Bible, the New Clarified Reference Bible—the one for which we almost lost the pictures in the fire. We sold $126,000 worth of them in less than a full year of operation. At the close of the second year, June 30,

1965, we recorded sales of $310,000. The following year that doubled to $625,000, and we still had just this one basic product. In 1967 we went well over the million mark with $1,221,000. Incredibly, in 1968 we were over $2.5 million.

Our shareholders seemed well pleased. Royal Publishers saw a nearly 100 percent increase each year from the previous year. People were beginning to say, "This guy, Sam Moore, can walk on water!" The stock they bought at four dollars a share became worth almost twice as much in just two or three years.

By 1967 we were short on capital again because we were still financing our own receivables. We decided to make a secondary stock offering, first to our shareholders. One of the people who bought this offering was Fred Wright, president of Wright Industries, and an outstanding Christian layman in Nashville. He became a director and bought ten thousand shares of stock.

Then Jack Massey came into my life. Fred Wright had said, "Let me tell you, Sam, Jack Massey is an honorable man, and he has capital. You should have him on your board." Fred arranged for me to meet Mr. Massey, who was also the chairman of Baptist Hospital in Nashville.

I had met Jack Massey briefly when we went public with Royal Publishers in 1962. At about that time he bought Kentucky Fried Chicken from Colonel Sanders. A few years later that company, which had cost him $2 million, sold for $250 million. Mr. Massey became the man with the golden touch, and he didn't start making big money until after he was sixty!

I went over to Baptist Hospital to meet him. I immediately loved Jack Massey—a great businessman, very smart, very wise—a man who took the time and interest in me and our company that made a difference. He liked my presentation and bought ten thousand shares of stock in the company. I told him I had ten thousand more shares but I had arranged to sell them to John J. and Henry Hooker.

To my surprise, neither of the Hooker brothers ever called me to follow through on the arrangement. I figured they had changed their minds, and let it go at that. Three days after the purchase date had come and gone, I went ahead and sold those additional shares to Mr. Massey.

Then John Hooker's brother, Henry, and Jack Massey happened to be on a plane together, and Jack was telling him about the company with serious enthusiasm. Henry looked at him and said, "Yes, my brother is already lined up to purchase ten thousand shares. He's just got to call Sam Moore."

Jack told him, "Don't call him. I bought them." Henry was very upset, and Jack was gracious enough to have a special board meeting. He voted to have an additional ten thousand shares available for John and his brother at seven dollars a share, the same price as Jack had paid. That wasn't in his own best interests, but that was the kind of guy Jack Massey was.

He became a partner of mine and invested in the company in 1967. He was a director from 1967 until 1991 when he passed away. Ours was the last public company he was involved with as a board member. Though he was past eighty and in a wheelchair, his mind was as sharp as a razor. It seemed to mean a lot to him to be able to continue on our board right up until his death. He is one of the most gifted businessmen who ever came to Nashville, and I was grateful to have his mentoring and expertise over the years.

John J. Hooker, who also served on our board, started Minnie Pearl Chicken and other businesses. He was very politically oriented and later ran, unsuccessfully, for governor and U.S. senator. So all in all, God gave us a wonderful blue-ribbon group of leaders to guide our fledgling company.

Unless the Lord builds the house, they labor in vain who build it. Psalm 127:1 (NKJV).

One of our bestselling authors, Dr. John Hagee in San Antonio, Texas 1997.

Above Right—I had the privilege of meeting New York Attorney Mayor David Deakins during a visit there in 1992.

The current Thomas Nelson board members. Standing from left to right: Brownlee O. Currey, Jr.; Joe M. Rodgers; W. Lipscomb Davis, Jr.; S. Joseph Moore; Millard V. Oakley; Robert J. Neibel, Sr. Seated from left to right: Andrew Young; Sam Moore; Cal Turner, Jr.

Mr. Richard Grasso president of the New York Stock Exchange, Joe Moore and myself at the NYSE on May 19, 1995. The day Thomas Nelson was listed on the big board !

Below—The day we bought Word Inc. From left, standing Phil Meek, senior vice president at Capitol Cities/ABC; Anne Maynard Gray, president of Diversified publishing group; Joe L. Powers, CFO at Thomas Nelson; Roland Lundy, president of Word , Inc. Seated, Sam Moore, president and CEO of Thomas Nelson; Ronald Doerfler, senior vice president and CFO Capital Cities/ABC.

Photo by: Steve Roebuck

Jack Massey and I share our blueprints with president Ronald Reagan as he helps us with our groundbreaking in the fall of 1980.

The Thomas Nelson building in 1997.

Varsity sales school summer of 1975.

A 1993 dinner with Tennessee's leaders. From left, Senator Jim Sasser, Sam Moore, Millard Oakley (a Thomas Nelson board member), Senator Harlan Matthews, and Governor Ned McWherter.

THE NELSON TEAM — 1970s

Joe Powers,
Financial Officer

Bernard Deeter,
Vice president of Sales

Robert J. Niebel,
Senior Vice President

Thomas Harris,
Vice President of Operations

Joe Ritchie,
Vice President International Sales

Bill Fox,
Sales Manager

Larry Stone,
Director of Advertising

Peter Gillquist,
Senior Editor

Helen Hozier,
Women's Books Editor

Varsity sales school summer of 1975.

Mama and me. Notice the warmth of her beautiful Christian smile.

Bottom Left—With my wife Peggy, son Joe, daughter-in law Julia, and their two children Ellery and Matthew Samuel in May of 1997.

Joe and Julia

In Seoul Korea, June 1983.

Peggy and I have a few moments with President George Bush and the first lady, Barbara.

Below Left—With my grandson, Timothy and daughter Sandra on July 4, 1989.

Below Right—With my daughter Rachel at Milligan College in Johnson City, TN, receiving an honorary Doctorate degree in Economics.

The five brothers from left to right, Sam, Mike, Tony, Chuck, and Kelly. Mom is in the middle.

A brief twenty-five years later my bride and I renewed our vows.

Right—How's this for a nice bunch of pheasants? A Saturday away from the office in 1983.

Sam, Peggy, Joe, Sandra, and Rachel

Left—Joe, at 16 months, and me outside our home in March 1964.

Below—Easter Sunday 1974. Joe 11, Sandra 6, Rachel 1.

Left—Me at age 25, in March of 1954.

Below—Mr. Devore, president of the International Book Company, is on the front row left and I'm in the middle. This is my summer sales team and some of their parents in the mid 1950s.

That's my brother Mike and my daughter Rachel during a visit in 1993 to our boyhood home.

Above—In 1954 I ran for student body president at Columbia Bible College. This is the campaign button photo.

Right—Here I am with a college friend, Barney Hatem. That famous '51 Chevy is in the background.

Our Wedding day October 25, 1958, in Johnson City, TN.

Chapter Nine

Enter Thomas Nelson

I t was toward the end of 1967 that I received a call from Charles Cridland, the president of Thomas Nelson and Sons in Camden, New Jersey, a company widely regarded as a world leader in Bible publishing. He asked if I would come and meet with him, which I did. Because of the success I was having with Royal Publishers, my marketing experience, and the fact that I understood accounting, he was hoping I could be persuaded to run the Thomas Nelson company. I told him I would like to meet Lord Thompson, the owner of the company.

Subsequently, I received a call from Lord Thompson himself in London. We spoke for a while, and he invited me to come and meet him in New York. I agreed, sensing a larger opportunity might be available. I had been praying about this since my meeting with Charles Cridland in Camden.

I told Jack Massey about the situation before I went. I really wasn't sure if they wanted to hire me or sell the company. When I got there I found out their interest was in hiring me to run the company. But Jack told me, "If you think you can buy the company, don't worry about the money. We'll come up with the cash."

Lord Thompson had a managing director by the name of Gordon Brunton. He was a very smart businessman who was running the Thompson organization. They owned Thomas Nelson worldwide, as well as various newspapers and many other enterprises around the world, including several TV stations. They had offices in England, Canada, the United States, and other countries

I was a bit nervous about meeting an English lord for the first time. I did not know how to properly address him. But I would learn. They sent two first-class tickets for Peggy and me to fly to New York. We met them at their hotel.

When I looked at the company profile and they showed me the statements for the previous year, I saw that Thomas Nelson had had total sales of only $1,442,000. Lord Thompson grew quiet and said to me, "I would like you to run our U.S. operation."

Back in 1962 Thomas Nelson U.S. had over $10 million in sales. Now in 1968 it had gone down all the way to $1.4 million. Central to the decline was the strategic failure to defend their exclusive right to publish the Revised Standard Version of the Bible (RSV). Five other publishers had swooped in and nearly decimated their business. They captured the market quickly, and Nelson was going down fast.

Royal Publishers, which had been in business only five years, did $2.5 million in 1967. So I looked at him and said, "Look, Lord Thompson, I run a small public company. It would be very difficult for me to leave my job and not support our shareholders. But let me ask you this. Would you be willing to sell?"

Mr. Brunton looked me in the eye and immediately said, "Son, Lord Thompson doesn't sell. He buys."

I looked back at him and said, "Sir, God made it such that sometimes we all have to sell."

Lord Thompson, a kind, gray-headed gentleman, looked at me squarely and asked, "Sam, do you have the money to buy the Thomas Nelson company?"

"I think so," I answered

He said, "It's four million dollars we want, and we must have it in cash."

"Sir, if it's worth four million you'll get it, and you'll get it in cash."

Getting to Yes

So we agreed I would study their books and examine all the records of the company. It wasn't until I went to the bindery in Camden and looked carefully at the plant and its books, that I discovered how bad things really were. After an audit and a review of the inventory, the receivables, the plates, and the factory and warehouse, it became apparent to us the company wasn't worth anywhere near the $4 million they were asking. However, it was worth $2 million.

At that time the English government was giving special bonuses to those who could bring U.S. dollars into Britain, because the pound was slipping. The government was giving something like a 25 percent bonus if a company could bring in dollars. So they definitely wanted it in cash.

We met again and I said to Lord Thompson, "Look, the company is not making enough to even justify the interest." We offered $2 million in cash. We expected they would turn that down, and they did.

When they lowered the price to $3 million I told them, "No, I cannot pay $3 million. We'd be willing to go up to $2.5 million." We settled on a final price of $2,640,000.

A few weeks before we bought the Thomas Nelson company, we sold one hundred thousand shares of Royal stock for nineteen dollars a share via Wiley Brothers, a local broker in Nashville. The shares were sold out in one day (they were over-subscribed—we could have sold many more), and the stock of Royal had moved in about five years' time from four dollars to nineteen dollars per share.

When we made this third offering of one hundred thousand shares at nineteen dollars, we raised $1,900,000 in cash. We were able to borrow a little more money and buy the company. We paid Lord Thompson $2 million down immediately in cash, and we paid the rest at the end of two years with interest.

How Thomas Nelson Came to Be

Let me tell you about the history of the Thomas Nelson company. I liked the fact that Thomas Nelson began in 1798, and I thought that the name itself, *Thomas Nelson*, conveyed a sense of history and expertise. Young Mr. Nelson, who at the age of nineteen started a small used bookstore in Edinburgh, Scotland, had grown it into a very large business. It reminded me of my story. I felt a connection between his early days and my own. Although his company was almost 160 years ahead of mine, it was a company I would like to have associated with mine.

It was the desire of Mr. Nelson that he publish books for the masses. He felt that if England were to rise, it would be because its people would read. Important books—especially Christian books—had to be readily and inexpensively available. I had the same feeling here in this country. If America was going to become a better nation, it needed more Christian books and Bibles at affordable prices. So we both were coming from the same angle.

Thomas Nelson published *The Pilgrim's Progress*. It was the first company that originated and popularized the *Strong's Concordance*. This is still, to this day, the classic concordance of our time. Many commentaries and other original products they created in the early days are still in wide use.

Thomas Nelson, the man, was born in 1780 near Stirling, Scotland, and his father was a farmworker. A gifted pupil in school, he at first leaned toward the idea of teaching.

Then his thoughts turned to the possibility of sailing to the West Indies to earn his fortune. From an unknown early biographer we learn the following:

> On a day preceding his planned departure this question was asked by his godly parent: "Thomas, my boy, have you ever thought that where you are going you will be far away from your means of grace?"
>
> The lad reflected and replied, "No, Father, I never thought of that. And I won't go." His response mirrored the deep hold that

Christian considerations had upon this young man's heart. At the last moment, he decided to stay home.

At first, Nelson undertook no original publishing, but simply printed and sold books and excerpts of books that were among his own favorite religious readings. Besides Bunyon's *Pilgrim's Progress* he also published Baxter's *Saints' Everlasting Rest.* He published such famous literary classics as the *Vicar of Wakefield, Robinson Crusoe,* and other books and essays. He did them one way: inexpensively.

Thomas Nelson was the first publisher to employ a salesman to call on bookstores. Mr. James MacDonald was the world's first publisher's representative.

In the 1830s, Nelson's two sons, William and Thomas Jr., came on board to help their father with his publishing efforts. Young Thomas was dispatched to London in the 1840s to open a branch operation, while his brother stayed behind on the south side of Edinburgh, to run the manufacturing operation. Through William's efforts in South Edinburgh, the first building housing the Thomas Nelson company was built in 1845 in an area called Hope Park.

By the early 1850s there were scores of employees. A south wing was added to the facility. Thomas Nelson was perhaps the largest publishing house in Scotland and had expanded his operation to include educational books, which were very well received.

With the business growing so rapidly, the younger Thomas Nelson voyaged to New York City in 1854, where he opened an office. This was another first: a British publisher establishing a branch office in the United States.

Again from an unknown biographer comes this gripping account of the end of Nelson's life:

> For the last five-and-twenty years of his life, Nelson was more or less of an invalid; though from 1843 to 1850 he enjoyed a kind of respite; but during this whole period his sons were associated with him in the business, and during the latter and greater portion of it, the management devolved entirely upon them. Thomas Nelson, the founder, died on March 23rd, 1861, and showed upon his deathbed the effects of that strong piety to which, since a child, he had accustomed his mind. When it was thought proper to announce to him that his end was near, he received the intelligence with the calmest equanimity:—"I thought so; my days are wholly in God's hands. He doeth all things well. His will be done!" and then he took up his Testament again, saying, "Now I must finish my chapter."

Imagine, the last earthly act of the man who founded the Thomas Nelson company—the largest Bible publisher in history—was to read again the Holy Scriptures!

At the time of his death, his two sons had the company well under control and employed almost six hundred people.

Company Guidelines

It was in 1865 that Thomas Nelson and Sons, Edinburgh, established a nine-point guide for employees shown on page 112. And I thought I was tough on my employees!

A tragic fire destroyed the Hope Park facility in April 1878, totally destroying the building and everything inside. Four

RULES AND REGULATIONS

OF

THE ESTABLISHMENT OF THOMAS NELSON AND SONS,

HOPE PARK, EDINBURGH.

I. The working-hours shall be 54 per week from this date.

II. The work-bell of the Establishment will be rung 5 minutes before each hour for resuming work, and the door of each Department will be opened at same time for the Workers.

III. The following Fines for Irregular Attendance will be exacted, namely:—Those whose wages are 20s. and upwards per week shall be fined 1½d. if not present at the respective hours for assembling; and those whose wages are under 20s. and not lower than 10s. per week, 1d.; and those whose wages are under 10s. per week, ½d. In addition to the foregoing, all under-time will be deducted.

IV. Workers absent an entire morning, forenoon, or afternoon, without permission, will be fined as follows:— Those on piece-work, whose wages average 15s. and upwards per week, 4d., and those whose wages are under 15s per week, 2d. Those on time at half these rates.

V. Individuals absenting themselves from work without giving intimation, and a sufficient reason therefor, by 11 o'clock of the day on which they are absent, will render themselves liable to the loss of their situations without receiving the usual notice.

VI. No Workers will be permitted to leave the premises during working-hours without having a pass from the Overseer of their Department.

VII. Individuals leaving the room in which they are employed before the work-bell has rung for dismissal will be fined 1d.

VIII. Persons habitually late in coming to work will render themselves liable to dismissal without the usual warning.

IX. Any waste of gas or materials will render those responsible for them liable to a fine, subject to the discretion of the Overseer.

HOPE PARK, Nov. 3, 1865.

hundred employees found themselves without work. Not to be defeated, the younger Thomas Nelson immediately ordered new printing presses and equipment from France and America, and hired an architect and builder for reconstruction.

Up and running within two months in a temporary facility, the publishing operation continued. Though the monetary loss was great, there was very little loss of momentum in the publishing work. The new permanent building reopened in 1880. Interestingly, a series of seventy educational books were introduced, known as the "Royal" series. It was yet another similarity between my background and theirs.

The Nelson publishing tradition continued as the next generation, the sons of Thomas and William, began to take over portions of the company by the early 1900s. With their participation, another new innovation was born. Mass-produced books measuring $4^{1}/_{4} \times 6^{1}/_{2}$ inches entered the market, thereafter to be known in the book trade as "Nelson size" books. These were reprints of traditional English classics and were very popular with readers. With this innovation, the practice of publishing for the masses as inexpensively as possible was continued. Today's "drugstore novel" format most likely is an outgrowth of this tradition.

Company growth in other operations outside England included branches in Paris and three warehouse operations throughout Canada, as well as growth in the United States. World War I slowed progress down considerably, but things began to pick up again after the war ended.

Thomas Nelson and Sons undertook its first Bible publishing venture in 1885 with their release of the King James Version. The Nelson edition was very popular, and this success set the stage for publishing newer translations. Next on the Nelson Bible list was the English Standard Version, published in 1887 and the famous American Standard Version, which was released in 1901.

In the 1940s, an agreement was reached whereby Thomas Nelson would have the exclusive right to publish the Revised Standard Version of the Bible (RSV), beginning with the New Testament in 1946. The entire RSV was published in 1952, and within two years nearly three million Bibles had been sold.

By 1960 the editorial offices in New York City were located on East 47th Street in midtown Manhattan.

In 1962 complaints were surfacing against the Thomas Nelson company for having the exclusive right to publish the RSV, but failing to meet the widespread demand for this product. Nelson had contracted originally for a ten-year exclusive plus a ten-year option, deriving these rights as a result of funding most of the translation and updating the American Standard Version of 1901 through the auspices of the National Council of Churches. The other Bible publishers would benefit if they could get some portion of that business, and they kept pressing for that opportunity.

In the end, the National Council of Churches decided to grant these other five publishers a license. As a result, Thomas Nelson, within a year, had five competitors instead of an exclusive proprietary arrangement on the RSV, and Nelson's sales began to plummet.

This explains why the company's revenues had shrunk from $10 million a year in wholesale volume to less than $2 million between 1963 and 1968. For that reason, Lord Thompson was very anxious to find new management and get things back on track. In my opinion, his business associates in England were not aware of the potential for the Bible business in America, nor did they fully comprehend the forces that made American Bible publishing successful. They were searching for someone who knew the market in America and thus the contact with me was initiated.

New Management

Many people were on hand to support us when we made the purchase. Mr. Ben Baiman had been executive vice president of World Publishing Company. Ben had retired earlier because of a heart attack. I asked him to be my adviser. At first he had counseled me against purchasing Thomas Nelson. He called it a "white elephant," a company riddled with bad customer problems and ill will. They often did not ship the RSV on time, and customers were frustrated. I listened, but disagreed.

After we bought the company, I asked Mr. Baiman to join our Thomas Nelson team, and he accepted. He was a great help to me in coming up with the design and long-term goals for our Bible line. One day I asked him, "Who would be the best person to help us develop our relationship with the trade?"

Without hesitation he recommended Bernard Deeter, who was at that time the vice president of World Publishing. Bernard decided to join us as president of Thomas Nelson with the mission to help develop a sales force for the trade and to design Bibles that would be acceptable to the marketplace.

I would continue on as president of Royal Publishers and Bernard would report to me. His operation was centered in Camden, New Jersey; and Royal continued on in Nashville. As you might guess, we shifted our efforts from door-to-door selling to servicing our nation's retail bookstores as our primary outlets.

Putting Together the Team

With the purchase of Thomas Nelson, we had an incredible increase in workload.

In business, I think it's a temptation as CEO to hire people just like yourself. For example, If I am fast on the draw and decisive, my tendency will be to look for executives who are by nature much like I am. But just the opposite is advisable: A good CEO needs to surround himself with people who will provide balance in the total company—people with a variety of gifts, a variety of talents, and even a variety of weaknesses.

One of the first people we hired in the late 1960s was Howard Utley, a CPA. He was a graduate of David Lipscomb in Nashville, an honest and careful manager who worked faithfully for me for many years. Howard introduced me to Tom Harris, and I found him while he was still in college at Lipscomb. Talk about fast on the draw, Tom was like a lightning bolt waiting to strike. He was born ready! He saw opportunities, and his mind raced ahead like a computer. Like a high school running back, he could do the hundred-yard dash in 9.7—with pads! When problems arose or barriers popped up, he operated on pure adrenaline and went into fast-forward. He was the classic type A personality.

The thing about Tom was, he was not always thorough. He was all offense, little defense. But he was fast, energetic, smart, a great motivator, and an outstanding manager. Ultimately, he became our vice president of production, later in charge of mergers and acquisitions, and a crucial part of our overall Thomas Nelson management team.

Shortly after Tom came on board, I hired Bob Niebel. I got his name from two short lists drawn up by friends at IBM and at Ernst & Ernst—his name came up on both lists. He was the chief financial officer of IKG Industries (which had been Rockwell Standard until they sold to Harsco Corp. in Harrisburg, Pennsylvania) here in Nashville. I had called Bob a couple of times without any luck. I called again and really pressed him to at least come and talk with me. He came over and after a couple of hours I convinced him to join us.

Bob Niebel invented thoroughness! He may be the most careful manager I have ever known. Before he makes a decision, he has to have absolutely all the facts. And then he still looks for more. And that's the wonderful difference between Bob and me.

I used to tell him, "Bob, you can't always wait until you have 100 percent of the facts. If you do, the opportunity we're considering will be gone." I would urge him to decide on the basis of as many facts as he could gather. He was so good and so thorough, he balanced our team. Tom was energy, Bob was efficiency. For years, Bob was senior vice president at Thomas Nelson, our chief operating officer.

When we needed a full-time financial officer, along came Joe Powers. Joe was also a Nashville product, having attended college at David Lipscomb. Joe Powers is great with people. Employees always feel comfortable with him. I have noticed over the years that he never says anything bad about anyone. He will either say something good or he won't say anything at all.

Joe never writes a nasty memo. He came to us as a first-class accountant and full of kindness for company employees—a double-edged sword. He is almost like the priest you seek out to make your confession. People were sometimes reluctant to come and talk with me, so they would instead touch base with Joe.

What a balance we had in these three men! I had one who saw things quickly and moved like lightning. I had another I knew I could count on to examine the facts. And I had one who knew the balance sheet of our company like no one else and was a peacemaker among the personnel.

As the company grew, I brought in my brother Chuck to run our Bible department. Talk about a new ledger sheet of talent, Chuck had earned his Ph.D. in chemistry. Later, he was on the team that had helped develop Excedrin for Bristol Myers. Further, he was an educator. He taught other people how to think. Chuck always finds a way to get things done. He manages the details and always has his section organized. But he's not a split-second decision maker. Or, to use our private lingo, he doesn't see the birds fast enough.

Chuck and I go hunting together. We try to go out on the opening day of dove season. We'll crouch down in the tall grass, maybe behind a fallen tree. When the birds come in, Chuck carefully lifts his gun, aims with precision, leading them just a bit, and readies himself for a clean shot. By contrast, the moment I see the birds, BOOM! And a couple fall to the ground. Chuck raises his hand and says, "Sam, you never give me a chance!"

That's the difference in us. I'm there to get birds. If I'm too precise, they're flying out of range while I wait for the perfect shot. A shell costs me only a few cents, but if I don't shoot, I miss my opportunity altogether. I can't buy another shot for any amount of money, so I take the chance. Chuck is more careful, but usually I bring in more birds.

I'm the same way in business. The reason I succeed, humbly speaking, is because I take the shots. I always remember my dad's advice, "Don't be afraid to take a chance." The difference between me and other people is that I often see the birds first and fire away in a split second. So you see how I need the Chuck Moores and the Bob Niebels of this world to balance me out!

A publishing company—or any company—cannot be run just by the editorial department, the n...rketing people, or the finance people. It has to be balanced. If you don't have strength in all these areas, you will fail. So instead of hiring people like me, I do just the opposite. The only person in those early years who was close to being like me was Tom Harris. With the balance of Bob Niebel, Chuck Moore, and Joe Powers to draw in the reins, we never made a business-ending or catastrophic mistake.

Evaluation

People ask me what I look for in conducting an interview, especially with a person on an executive level. For me, number one is mission: Where do you want to be in five years?

The second is skill. Does he or she have the brain power to get the job done? I ask the candidate, "What are you good at? What do you do best?" When I check the references, I ask former employers that same question about the candidate.

Hopefully the answers will correlate. If the one being interviewed brings an outstanding strength to a segment of our company where help is needed, this may well be the person I will hire. Ultimately I have to get a positive answer to the question, will this candidate perform in such a way as to increase shareholder value?

Third, does the applicant really want the job? Is the desire and attitude there to get it done? To me, there is a huge difference between what a person knows and what he or she desires to accomplish. I am willing to take a risk on the person who has the guts and the willingness to get up and go. A lazy man or woman can never be successful. I want someone with energy, fire in the belly, and a fierce desire to succeed.

Fourth, I look for loyalty. I want people who are loyal to me, loyal to the company, loyal to our overall goals, and loyal to the shareholders.

While I'm at it, let me take a moment and talk about shareholders. These are real people, friends, and neighbors down the block. Some of them are teachers, some retired people, many of them elderly, some are young parents investing for the future of their children's education. And you can't mess up when you are managing other people's money. It's a trust, like managing the widow's mite. As a corporate executive, I look out for our investors. I watch for new employees who are loyal to the owners of this company and can bring a return on their investment in Thomas Nelson, Inc.

This kind of care towards shareholders gets translated into management style. It means you become a bird-dog for efficiency, that you let people go (read: downsize) when they are inefficient. That's often followed by a charge that the CEO is hard-nosed or insensitive. It is precisely at this point that I face tension as a Christian. Where is the balance between compassion for trusting shareholders and compassion for struggling employees? For the boss, love for God must never become synonomous with being Milquetoast. Or to put it another way, I must not become so heavenly minded that I am no earthly good.

When I do an interview and probe for a person's skills, intellect, desires, and loyalty, loyalty is the toughest thing to spot. So I usually ask about the past record of the applicant, what he accomplished at his previous position and why he left. Does he bad-mouth that company and the people with whom he worked? Is he loyal only to himself, or also to others? In reality, you never know for sure whether a person is loyal or will succeed until he or she is on the job for a few months.

Loyalty is also fostered by the employer trusting the employee. When you trust people, they know you believe in them. Then they become loyal to you because they don't want to disappoint you. Furthermore, I find that when people believe in the cause that Thomas Nelson represents, they become far more loyal. Finally, loyalty grows when you compensate your people for their work. When I see a job well done, I pay extra for it in stock, cash, salary increase—or all three. People become disloyal very quickly when they feel they have been had. If I do a good job, I want to be paid for it.

One last thing. In my desire to succeed, I tend not to be very patient. This shows up in another of my weaknesses: I'm not a very good listener. So I make an effort to get together quite often with people reporting to me. My goal is to meet with my key executives several times a year one-on-one. I also make it a point to spend time with our management team and their spouses socially at least once a year. I listen to learn what the problems are. Then I seek to talk these problems through as friends.

I thank God for the incredible team we had in those early years. Of that original cast, Bernard Deeter passed away in 1996, Bob Niebel has retired and is still on our board, Tom Harris has moved to the West Coast and is with another company, and Joe Powers and Chuck Moore remain with the company, sharing my load to this very day.

And in the wings is an outstanding cadre of young men and women who will carry us well into the twenty-first century.

Chapter Ten

The Bible Business

One of the great disadvantages of an immigrant to America is that he or she struggles so much with the English language. But for me, this was an advantage. Everything I read had to be extremely clear in order for me to understand it. It was my dream from the beginning of my business days to help average people better understand the Holy Scriptures.

My education at Columbia Bible College and Seminary gave me a working knowledge of the Bible, and I was a committed Christian. But many of the people publishing the Bible in the 1960s weren't folks who actually took the Bible all that seriously in their daily lives. By and large they were not involved in disciplined daily study of the Scriptures. All they did was print it and sell it. Bible publishing was merely a business. Few were thinking about what the person buying the Bible might like to know and understand.

For example, someone might want to purchase a youth Bible for a young person, or a study Bible for a college student.

Children might like a smaller Bible that wasn't so big and heavy to carry around. An elderly lady might benefit from a large-print edition, and a pastor might be able to use a Bible with comprehensive teaching aids when sermon preparation time is at hand.

I knew that in launching our new Bible projects I had to have a strong central purpose, a singleness of vision and mission. In short, I decided to be a winner in one thing. What was my purpose? To be the best Bible publisher in the whole wide world. In fact, my goal was that in less than ten years I would combine Thomas Nelson and Royal Publishers to be that number one Bible publisher.

In 1971 Thomas Nelson held the publishing rights to the revered American Standard Version of 1901 (ASV), the Revised Standard Version (RSV), the old King James Version (KJV), which was modified and updated with Dr. Gutzke's notes, and the widely used Confraternity of Christian doctrine, the Roman Catholic translation.

In meeting with Ben Baiman, Bernard Deeter, and other Nelson executives, we decided we would focus on publishing these four translations and zero in carefully on meeting the needs of the consumer. Therefore, we wanted to publish editions of the Bible that the average customer could afford, just as our namesake had. We would offer Bibles that held value for the consumer and offered the greatest amount of accessible biblical knowledge.

The Giant Print Bible

We decided we would begin to fulfill our publishing goal with the publication of the Giant Print Bible.

Printing plates are made from film. The film negatives for a pulpit Bible with giant letters intended for public reading from church lecterns were hanging in the storage vault at the bindery in Camden, New Jersey. We inherited them along with everything else when we bought the company. Our Giant Print Bible would be created using this old set of negatives from that huge King James Version pulpit Bible.

We decided to reduce the size of the pages so the typeface would be a bit smaller than the pulpit Bible size. At the reduced size, what the printing industry calls "18-point type," the letters would come out about the size of those on a large dinner menu at a good restaurant, and easy to read. The letters would be noticeably larger than normal book-size print. This Giant Print edition was for individual readers who had a difficult time reading small print. If you are fifty or older, you know exactly what I mean!

Today we would call this idea a "no-brainer." But back then this was revolutionary within the industry. We would publish it in a "study size," $6^{1}/_{4} \times 9^{1}/_{4}$ inches, but to keep the thickness of the book down we printed it on very thin paper. This was the first time that Kingsport Press was willing to use nineteen-pound paper on a study-size book with heavy ink. All those evenings in the pressroom would now begin to pay big dividends.

To this Giant Print Bible we also added certain other features. We took the translation notes Dr. Gutzke had prepared and put them at the end of each verse. You would be reading the King James Version with the meaning of difficult words entered at the end of each verse. It was a huge job for us to "strip in" all of these interpretive words, but it was well worth the effort.

Other features were added, too, like the topical running heads on each page, the monies, weights, and measures charts, the Harmony of the Gospels, a concordance, and a selection of maps of the Holy Land.

Once the Giant Print Bible was ready, we took a risk on the upside with an initial print run of 50,000 copies. Thankfully, the first printing was sold before the book was even finished. So we did a second printing of 100,000 and soon thereafter a third printing of another 100,000. Within the first few months we had a best-seller on our hands.

People asked me, "Sam, how did you know this Bible would sell so well?"

First, we reasoned that it is older people who read the Bible regularly. In their later years people get serious about God, and retired people have more time to read the Scriptures daily. This was a Bible they could see to read. Next, we figured that many pastors who study the Scriptures regularly are certainly in that middle-aged to senior bracket. Furthermore, I wanted to help grandmothers read the Bible to their grandchildren. Once we thought it through, we were sure the Giant Print Bible would succeed far beyond market expectations.

The Varsity Program

I never could get selling books and Bibles door-to-door out of my blood. That training had been so good for me. So it was a natural that when I started my own Bible publishing business, we would certainly have a part of the company that would be devoted to door-to-door sales.

In 1971 I hired a wonderful man, Willard Hooberry, to start Varsity. We let go of the National Book Company name, and in 1971 we restarted the door-to-door sales operation as the Varsity Company, selling the Royal Family Bible and our own Clarified Reference Study Bible.

About this time, the Southwestern Company in Nashville, which recruited college kids to sell Bibles door-to-door, was changing hands. The new president brought in some of his own people. As a result, several Southwestern managers left the company, and a few of their top people joined us, including Frank Miller, Eddie Parker, and Dave Maddox. Then a "young rebel" named Sonny Crews came on the scene at Varsity. Sonny began his rise to the top from day one, and today he heads the entire Varsity operation.

The Varsity Company provides hundreds of college students each summer the opportunity to do essentially what I did when I was in school. In the tradition of major league baseball, I call Varsity the "Thomas Nelson farm program." We interview the kids, train them, show them how to manage their finances and their lives better, and we teach them priority and time management. If they grow into being good managers, if they can sell and meet the public well, we sometimes hire them after four or five successful summers and bring them into the company.

If a student shows unusual promise, we might help him or her through graduate school. Upon completion of that work, if there is room in the company, we may bring them on; otherwise we try to help them find a job elsewhere.

Each year it is my privilege to speak at the victory banquet of the Varsity effort at the end of each summer. Not only do the students come back to Nashville for this event, but many of their parents join us as well. I talk with the students about how God has become real to me in my personal life, how He guides me in my business, and how important it is for all of us to have Jesus Christ at the very center of our lives. Not only have we produced some wonderful salespeople out of this effort, but also a number of newly committed Christians as well.

Today we have several good managers working with Sonny: Rodney Dye, Roger McConnell, Glenn Ransom, Ramesh Retnam, and Leon Church, and a host of young, bright men and women such as Lisa Ward, Kevin Oh, Sarah Ng, Tom Tison, Matt Kahn, Paul Crain, Wayne Smith, Timmy Derusha, Julian Fawk, Nicole Everhart, Raphael Cordoso, and Mark Corwin.

The Open Bible

In 1972, after the Giant Print Bible was up and running, I turned my attention to my next project, the Open Bible. This was an edition that I worked on personally, designing many of the study helps in my office at home. I worked many nights until 2:00 A.M. designing the pages, adding the helps, the introductions to each book, the outlines of each book of the Bible, and generally deciding what would go where.

This was not the first study Bible to be published, to be sure. What I wanted to design was a Bible that had more notes for the common person than anything that had been published up until that time. So, in addition to the various notes and helps that accompanied each book, we also included the cyclopedic reference section, maps, table of weights and measures that were used in the ancient world, and cross references, which tell the reader where themes in one book of the New Testament, for example, are repeated in other books of the Bible.

The Open Bible made its debut in the retail marketplace at the Christian Booksellers Association (CBA) trade show in 1972. It was an immediate success among Bible students. Both Christian and secular bookstores ordered it in large quantities. Now published in several translations, it has become one of the most successful study Bibles ever.

By 1975, Thomas Nelson became the leading publisher of Bibles in the world. In fact, we published more Bibles than numbers two and three combined. Our original goal was to gain that position in ten years, but by the grace of God it took us only five. For me, this was a dream come true.

The New King James Version

In 1973 an event took place that not only changed my life but changed the direction and scope of Thomas Nelson Publishers. My son, Joe, was eleven years old and had made a decision to live for Christ. He was baptized by Dr. Frank Paschal at First Baptist Church in Nashville, and was given a New English Bible as a gift. But he ended up in a Sunday school class where everyone used the traditional King James Bible. They had memorized passages out of the King James and simply did not want to relearn verses from another translation. Most Christians using the King James Version in those days felt the same way.

For years I saw the King James Version as a beautiful and accurate translation for the time in which it was first published.

But now, hundreds of years later, it had become extremely difficult to understand. This was my concern when I first went to
Dr. Manford Gutzke to find a way to make the KJV text more
understandable.

Even back when I was studying the Old Testament under
Dr. Frank Sells at Columbia Bible College, I frequently became
frustrated trying to complete my reading assignments. It was
maddening to come upon sections in the KJV like the one in
Genesis where Pharaoh is describing his famous prophetic
dream to Joseph.

> AND, BEHOLD, THERE CAME UP OUT OF THE RIVER SEVEN KINE, FATFLESHED
> AND WELLFAVOURED; AND THEY FED IN A MEADOW: AND, BEHOLD, SEVEN
> OTHER KINE CAME UP AFTER THEM, POOR AND VERY ILL FAVOURED AND LEAN-
> FLESHED, SUCH AS I NEVER SAW IN ALL THE LAND OF EGYPT FOR BADNESS:
> AND THE LEAN AND THE ILL FAVOURED KINE DID EAT UP THE FIRST SEVEN FAT
> KINE.
>
> (GEN. 41:18–20 KJV)

I tried to find out what *kine* meant. The word wasn't in the
dictionary, and my roommate didn't know what *kine* meant
either. So I went back to Professor Sells and asked him, "How
do you know the meaning of that word?"

"It's Old English," he said, "and someone had to explain it
to me too! *Kine* means cows."

"That's not fair," I said. "It means I have to learn two
languages: the American language plus the King James language.
And I'm having a hard enough time with the one."

He laughed and told me, "That's the way it is, Sam."

But deep down it really bothered me, and I wasn't going to

let it go. I was determined to do something to help laypeople understand the Bible. So many of the words were old and obsolete.

Because Joe wanted a Bible like everyone else in his Sunday school class I gave him a King James Version. It was a beautiful leather edition, and I had his name embossed on the cover in gold. When I presented it to Joe, I recalled what Dr. Sells had said to me: That's the way it is.

About a month later, eleven-year-old Joe asked to talk with me one Sunday evening. I was sitting at my desk in my office at home, and he brought his new Bible into the room with him and laid it on the corner of my desk.

"Dad, I like this Bible you gave me. It's pretty. But I don't understand it."

He left the Bible on my desk and turned around to walk out of the office. He stopped for a moment and looked back at me. "Dad, with all the Bibles you publish, do you make one I can understand?"

I knew he was right, but his comments still stunned me. It was like a bombshell exploding in my head. I couldn't sleep that night. At two o'clock in the morning I was on my knees praying, "O God, how many people are there like my son, Joe, who read the Bible but don't understand what it means?"

I decided then and there to do something about it. That may be "the way it is," but it doesn't have to remain that way. The next morning, I telephoned my old Sunday school teacher, Maxie Jarman, chairman of Genesco, the huge shoe manufacturing company. Maxie was "Mr. Nashville." He was a highly acclaimed Christian in so many different circles, and I had a great personal admiration for him.

I told Mr. Jarman about my conversation with Joe. I could just see him shaking his head in consternation when he said, "That's right, Sam. The King James Bible is a great translation, but for most of today's population it's obsolete."

"How can we do something about that?" I asked him.

We were both at a loss to come up with a solution there on the spot. So many people were "married" to the KJV, so how in the world could you change the unchangeable?

Another Christian friend of mine in Nashville, a man very prominent in Gideons International (the folks who put the Bibles in your hotel room), was John Leeson. We had been discussing this for some time at church in the adult men's Sunday school class in Mt. Juliet. We had moved our membership from First Baptist downtown to First Baptist Mt. Juliet, which was five minutes away from home. Our second child, Sandra Lee, was six years old. Our baby, Rachel Michelle, was about a year old, and it was so much easier with three children to be close to church. I had told John that I would love to have a Bible that was truly the King James Version, but updated into the language we use and understand today. John felt the same way Maxie Jarman and I did. It was time to take action.

I asked John Leeson and Frank Hiam, director of the Bible division at Thomas Nelson, to visit some of the leading biblical scholars of the day and find out if there would be any serious professional interest in doing a new version or an update of the King James Version. They visited schools such as Dallas Seminary, Biola (Talbott), Conservative Baptist Seminary in Denver, Golden Gate in San Francisco, Seattle Pacific, and Trinity in suburban Chicago.

During that same general period of time, I had been at a

hotel in Detroit with Dr. Elmer Towns, my college friend and now dean of Liberty University Seminary in Lynchburg, Virginia. Elmer also felt the time had come to update the King James Version. I shared the story about my son and the King James Bible I'd given him.

"What we need to do is to take the King James and keep its beauty, keep it the same where it is accurate, and retain its warmth because it is lodged in the hearts of people," he said. "But let's bring it into the twentieth century." He agreed to help in any way he could.

I had spoken with Dr. Arthur Farstad, a professor of New Testament Greek at Dallas Theological Seminary and a brilliant scholar, and he was very enthusiastic about wanting to be involved with this project too. Like each of us, he felt strongly it was time to do something to make the King James Version more accessible to the average Christian. This was an exciting development for him, and he yearned for direct involvement.

So here were a number of godly men of very different backgrounds—an outstanding business executive employing over sixty thousand people, an active Gideon, a number of scholars and professors, and me, a publisher—and we all felt the same way. That beautiful old translation called the King James Version must be made more understandable.

It's important to mention here that the King James Version has had a number of typographic revisions earlier in its history. This means old-style letters and words were updated. For example, if you were to find the original version, much of it would be in that old English where a *w* was still rendered as a *uu*, and where the letter *s* was rendered more like an *f*. We were proposing a linguistic revision, retranslating words from the ancient

Greek texts into more modern English. Our revision would go much farther than these earlier updates had gone.

Maxie Jarman, John Leeson, and I decided the next step would be to call together a committee of Christian scholars and leaders to ascertain what level of interest there would be in a newly updated version of the KJV. I wanted to be sure the Christian market would be open and accept this new Bible. So I made a number of calls myself to leading pastors across the country. The consensus was, yes, the King James needed to be updated, and it would be wonderful if someone could find a way to do it.

In order to ensure that we would be meeting the needs of public worship, Christian education, and personal reading, study, and memorization, I decided to call a conference—in fact two conferences—one to be held in Nashville, the other in Chicago. We invited about seventy-five outstanding Christian leaders from around the country—men and women, clergy, scholars, and laity—to come at our expense to one of these two conferences to discuss and plan this important project.

Starting in the fall of 1975 and continuing through the end of that year, I set up what would come to be known as the North American Overview Committee. Here is a partial list of those who participated between the two locations: Dr. B. Clayton Bell, Rev. D. Stuart Briscoe, Dr. Robert Coleman, Dr. W. A. Criswell, Mrs. Mary C. Crowley, Mrs. Millie Dienert, Dr. Jerry Falwell, Very Rev. Peter E. Gillquist, Rev. William S. Glass, Dr. Ben Haden, Dr. Richard Halverson, Dr. Howard G. Hendricks, Dr. E. V. Hill, Dr. D. James Kennedy, Dr. Jay Kesler, Dr. Tim F. LaHaye, Dr. Harold Lindsell, Dr. David L. McKenna, Dr. J. Robertson McQuilken, Dr. Jess C. Moody,

Dr. Harold J. Ockenga, Dr. Lloyd John Ogilvie, Rev. Luis Palau, Dr. J. Dwight Pentecost, Dr. John R. Rice, Dr. Adrian P. Rogers, and Dr. Elmer Towns.

I asked Dr. Arthur Farstad to make a presentation to the other scholars at these conferences concerning the need for the King James Version to be updated. The response was overwhelmingly positive and I invited Dr. Farstad to become the interim editor for the New Testament portion of the Scripture.

I had purposely invited many conservative leaders to join us, men such as Dr. W. A. Criswell, Dr. Jerry Falwell, Dr. John R. Rice, Dr. J. Vernon McGee, and Dr. J. Dwight Pentecost, sensing they would be least likely to want to tamper with the KJV. To my amazement and joy, these men also believed the venerable old King James Version needed to be updated.

In mid-1975, Maxie Jarman came to me and said, "Since the King James Bible came out of England, would it not make sense to try to pull a group of English Bible scholars together in London to get their opinion, on an update?"

Early in 1976 I set up the meeting of what would come to be known as the Commonwealth Overview Committee. We met at the Royal Dorchester Hotel in London with a number of British scholars, and their conclusion was the same as those who met in the United States. Participants included: Sir Cyril Black, Rev. Raymond Brown, Rev. David B. Bubbers, Prof. William J. Cameron, Mr. Donald J. Crowther, Mr. Edward England, Dr. James William Fairbairn, Rt. Rev. A. W. Goodwin-Hudson, Mr. David R. L. Porter, Sir J. Eric Richardson, Rev. David H. Wheaton, and Rt. Rev. Maurice A. P. Wood.

Of the many resolutions that came out of the three meetings, perhaps the most far-reaching was the determination that *thee* and *thou,* along with the obsolete forms of verbs (com*eth,* look*est,* and believ*eth*) that go with them, would not be used in this new version. As a direct result of these meetings a committee of scholars was formed to do the update and the project began in earnest shortly thereafter.

Our modus operandi was quite simple, though the project itself was far more work than any of us had initially imagined. Art Farstad was chosen to head the New Testament editorial committee, while Dr. James Price of Tennessee Temple University headed the work on the Old Testament, ably assisted by Dr. William White. Each scholar was assigned one or more books and editorial guidelines were adopted as to how the work would proceed. The scholars collectively met periodically with Bob Sanford, our able director of Bible Editorial to decide on the tone and the kind of language the finished product would use. Then they proceeded to work individually on their translation.

Ultimately, the translation was standardized from book to book. The revised manuscript of each book from both the Old and New Testaments was sent to several reviewers, and a careful and thorough process involving the translator, our esteemed English editor Dr. William H. McDowell, and other scholars assured us everything was in order. Then the last draft was submitted to a handpicked group of scholars who did the final polishing of the text.

I decided as a final step to establish an Executive Review Committee (ERC). The team of scholars and my executive editors thought I was "gilding the lily" here, but I wanted to be sure we had the very best possible manuscript before going ahead with publication. After we completed the executive review process, all agreed it had been a worthwhile step. Additional important matters came to light and were addressed, making the final draft even better. Fittingly, the work was completed in founder Thomas Nelson's own country of Scotland, where the ERC spent a month in St. Andrews poring over the final manuscript. The New King James Version of the Bible was completed and delivered to our warehouse in Nashville in August 1982.

It was an awesome and humbling experience. One of my personal goals had been to not interfere with the work of the committees. This new version was shaped by the many learned and gifted people God provided. The process was not unlike the one that had yielded the original King James Version in 1611. My three trusted decision makers and personal advisers were Arthur Farstad, James Price, and Batsell Barrett Baxter. Dr. Baxter reviewed every word of the New Testament. He was one of the most godly and humble scholars I ever knew.

By the beginning of 1998 the New King James Version has sold approximately thirty million copies in all of its editions. For many years, it was the number two Bible in America, right next to the KJV. We believe acceptance of the NKJV by the Christian public will become even wider and endure for many, many years. For me, personally, it is the most important project we as a company have ever done.

At the time of its two-hundredth anniversary, the Thomas Nelson company is the leader worldwide in Bible publishing. It is as though we have come full circle, back to what originally was a company known for its Christian book and Bible reference publishing. I'm bold enough to believe Mr. Thomas Nelson himself would have been very proud!

Chapter Eleven

The Book Business

God has blessed me greatly in allowing me the privilege of working with many wonderful ministries around the world. For thirty years Thomas Nelson has helped hundreds of ministries raise money for their radio, television, and other outreach programs by creating customized Bibles, books, and gift products. Each of these items is offered by the various ministries we serve for a donation that funds their work for Christ.

Over the years it has been my observation even in the midst of various circumstances and troubling situations, God's grace abounds and He continues to bless ministries and churches of all sizes. I am so thankful that in our relationships with ministries and churches we have assisted in raising billions of dollars to spread the gospel message.

Two projects are especially memorable. The first is "Project Pearl." In 1979 our company produced over one million Chinese Bibles for Open Doors with Brother Andrew. This huge campaign of bringing Bibles into Communist China was a major challenge and extremely dangerous. With God's protection, Open Doors accomplished their mission, and to this day Chinese people are accepting Christ from the seeds that were planted with those one million Bibles.

Another close relationship is with Dr. Jerry Falwell and the "I Love America" campaign. We produced customized Bibles and books for Dr. Falwell. In the "I Love America" rallies, Dr. Falwell and Liberty students talked about how we all needed to rise up and rekindle our love for America and return to the biblical principles upon which it was founded. As an immigrant to America, this campaign was very meaningful to me.

There are so many other special people. In the early 1970s, I met Dr. W. A. Criswell, pastor of First Baptist Church in Dallas. Dr. Criswell, the "prince of preachers," was the general editor of the *Criswell Study Bible* we published several years ago. Also, Dr. J. Vernon McGee became a close personal friend. He had a radio program that helped instruct believers to live out the Word of God. I urged him to put his message in print to provide believers with a greater study resource. The result was *Thru the Bible Commentary.*

Oral Roberts is also a good friend. It was an honor to publish his autobiography, *Expect a Miracle.* Pastor Jack Hayford has been helping us with his work as general editor for *The Spirit Filled Life Bible.*

Robert Schuller, Charles Stanley, Chuck Swindoll, John Hagee, Billy Graham, D. James Kennedy, Beverly and Tim La-Haye, and James Dobson are just a few of the hundreds of pastors and leaders we have worked with that have helped change the world for Christ. Others come to mind as well—O. S. Hawkins, Paige and Dorothy Patterson, Jack Graham,

Billie Friel and Frank Paschal, my pastors for over thirty years in Nashville, and Keith Thomas, our pastor in Florida. With over 6,000 ministries and hundreds of thousands of churches, each one has worked at fulfilling the Great Commission and impacting lives to the glory of God.

I love this part of the business as well as the opportunity to travel with Ted Squires, the Vice President of Nelson Resource Management, his account representatives and other salespeople to meet with pastors and evangelists and determine how God might have us work together. Ted has a knack for knowing when to contact these leaders. If one statement could summarize the many years of working side by side with these gifted individuals called of God, it would be this: people have blessed and enriched the lives of millions through the gospel of Jesus Christ, and I have been given the privilege to work side by side with these men and women.

The Bicentennial Almanac

By 1975, with such wonderful success in our Bible publishing venture, I wanted to turn my attention to book publishing. An attainable goal, I believed, would be to develop the finest Christian book publishing effort in America. But first, there was a bit of unfinished business for me.

The two-hundredth anniversary of the founding of America was upon us, and this "American by choice" wanted to have something to offer our country that would extol the richness of her history. If you remember, we had just come off a decade or so of rampant anti-Americanism. Critics tended to emphasize what was wrong with America.

Let me be clear in saying that I do not buy the slogan "America, Right or Wrong." There are times we need to voice our opposition to government policy. I myself am a critic of abortion on demand, which has swept through our culture much the same as the Nazi Holocaust smothered Europe nearly two generations ago. We are weaker than we care to admit in the area of race relations. And I still believe that God expresses His image in us by creating people male and female. So this patriot is not mindlessly loyal no matter what.

In early 1975, with the bicentennial approaching, I sensed it was time for somebody to publish a book that would emphasize the accomplishments of America over the past two hundred years. A manuscript called *The Bicentennial Almanac* was made available to Thomas Nelson for publication. There was nothing you would call special about the *Almanac*—it just took our two hundred years of history and highlighted the major events that took place, year by year. The editor, Calvin D. Linton, Ph.D., had done a thorough and rather unbiased job of summarizing American history. I believe he came to us because he felt the market for his book might be more in door-to-door sales rather than in the bookstores. We enthusiastically offered him both.

We took a look at the manuscript and asked, "How can we make this even better?" The decision was made to fill the book with a generous array of black-and-white and color photos, engravings, works of American art, maps, and other graphic material to make the text even more alive.

When I said I was willing to publish the book, Dr. Linton said he would prefer full payment as opposed to royalties and we signed the contract. Once the project was in-house, we spent a great deal more on film work, and made additional investments for further editorial work.

Over the course of 1975 things changed dramatically in America. We were unaware when we made the publishing decision on the Almanac that President Richard Nixon would face impeachment hearings for his alleged involvement in Watergate. By the time he offered his resignation that summer, we had sunk more than $100,000 into the book and wondered if we would have to write it off as a loss. Because of the political problems engulfing our nation, most publishers simply forgot the bicentennial.

The one that didn't was this spunky outfit in Nashville, Tennessee, Thomas Nelson, Inc. Not only did we have the best product for the bicentennial, we had virtually the only product. Harold Leach did a first-class job on production, and Bill Fox marshalled the sales force to place it in the stores.

The Bicentennial Almanac became the hottest commodity on American bookstore shelves. More than 600,000 copies were sold at $19.95 in hardcover—with no royalties! Even someone who struggled through Econ. 101 could tally up this sort of profit. Just when we needed a massive capital infusion to complete the New King James Version, here was the runaway success of *The Bicentennial Almanac.*

Again, it probably takes an immigrant to occasionally remind the rest of the country what a wonderful place we have in which to live. This is my country now. I wanted to toot the horn for my adopted home. We had our Watergate, and unfortunately there will be other scandals as well. But the big picture is, there is no place on earth I would rather live.

The Christian Book Program

While *The Bicentennial Almanac* was essentially a secular book, my heart's desire was to launch out into the deep and begin a division of the company committed solely to the publication of Christian books. We had done a number of children's books, some outstanding reference works, cookbooks, even dictionaries. Once we had gained such strong momentum in the publication of Bibles, I also wanted us to be the number one supplier of Christian books to the retail bookstores of America.

We already had two very bright advertising people, Larry Stone and Jim Powell, who were also gifted in editorial planning. But I needed somebody to head our Christian book effort.

I had heard about Peter Gillquist and had invited him to be part of the Overview Committee for the New King James edition of the Bible. He majored in journalism at the University of Minnesota, had a seminary background, and was a leader in Campus Crusade. He came for an interview in mid-1975, having written two successful books himself. And he had just finished working with country music superstar Johnny Cash on the editing of his landmark autobiography, *Man in Black*.

When Peter signed on with Thomas Nelson, I called him in, along with Larry Stone, and we set our goals: ten outstanding books the first year, twenty the second. Peter immediately signed up several people who became our successful authors— Chuck Swindoll, Jody and Linda Dillow, Dr. Jack Sparks, and Joyce Landorf. We were on our way.

Soon Helen Hosier came on board to specifically work with books for women. Bruce Nygren became our very dependable in-house editor. More memorable books were published by authors such as Dr. Robert Schuller, Dr. Maurice Rawlings, Katherine Koob, and J. Vernon McGee.

Larry Stone did the research to discover the twelve best Christian book markets in America. We decided to take our authors on a tour to meet with the booksellers in their own cities and talk about the publishing philosophy of Thomas Nelson. We made a commitment to publish books that reflected four characteristics: *honesty, quality, orthodoxy,* and *validity.* We wanted to distribute books that were not only consistent with biblical Christianity, but were also written to be understandable to common readers—just like the notes in our Bibles!

Because of the success of our early book lists and the tremendous amount of time and money we invested in advertising and promotion, soon established Christian authors were coming to us asking if we would be their publisher. They liked the fact that we worked to place Christian books not just in religious outlets, but in secular stores too. The book program began to grow significantly, and soon we added other key personnel: Wendy Ragan ran the office while Peter was out looking for more authors, and Janet Thoma found authors to write Christian children's books.

The New American Bible

Of course our Bible publishing continued to grow as well. By 1976 we had become successful with the New American Bible (NAB), a very clear and understandable Roman Catholic translation. Because it was so well received, we decided to accept an invitation to present the NAB to the Roman Catholic hierarchs at the Eucharistic Conference in Philadelphia in the fall of 1976. I asked Peter Gillquist and Larry Stone to join me on that trip. We had one thousand copies of the NAB specially bound, a pure white copy for the Holy Father in Rome, and one thousand other copies in beautiful tan leather, hand-numbered in sequence for each of the cardinals and bishops present from across America and the world.

A most memorable event was when thousands of people gathered at Veteran's Stadium for a Catholic charismatic praise and preaching event. Songs like "We Are One in the Spirit," "He Touched Me," and "God and Man at Table Are Sat Down" came as a pleasant surprise to our non-Roman Catholic ears. The Holy Spirit is indeed present in all places and fills all things!

But the most humorous highlight of that trip took place on our second day in Philadelphia at the home of the late John Cardinal Krol. At a dinner that evening, we were to present the special Bibles to the various hierarchs. The Bibles had been packed and shipped in scores of very heavy cardboard boxes, and numbered consecutively one to one thousand.

Just before the public presentations were to be made, a deacon approached me and said, "Mr. Moore, these are numbered editions, is that correct?"

I nodded yes.

"So you mean they go, for example, from 101 to 200, 201 to 300, and so forth?"

"That's right," I answered.

"When we get into the 600s," he continued, "everything is consecutive there as well?"

I couldn't figure out what he was getting at.

"I presume this means that there is a number 666," he said, finally making his point. "Mr. Moore, if that volume could be culled out, I'd really appreciate it!"

I had never seen Peter Gillquist and Larry Stone move so quickly as when they went through the boxes. They found the middle 600s and purged out this spurious and unwanted volume of the NAB. We laughed about it together on the plane the next day on the way back to Nashville. But I'm glad that persistent deacon had the courage to ask me about it, and save some poor bishop from inadvertantly receiving the dreaded number of the beast!

By the late 1970s the Christian book division was growing so rapidly that Peter Gillquist asked me if he could devote his time uniquely to acquisitions, and if Larry Stone could be brought in from advertising to head the administrative end of things. Others were hired as well to meet the growing demands in editorial and production.

In 1986 Peter Gillquist left the company to become a full-time priest in the Antiochian Orthodox Church, and soon Larry Stone departed and, with Ron Pitkin, developed their own successful publishing venture, Rutledge Hill Press. Dr. Victor Oliver had come with the company and helped fill this void as he developed new authors under the Oliver-Nelson imprint. The departure of Peter and Larry marked the end of a pioneering era for us, and laid a solid foundation for the next stage in our growth and development.

New Leadership

I received a phone call from a young man named Robert Wolgemuth. I knew him to be a person of great integrity and class, and he comes from a family with those same characteristics. His father, Sam Wolgemuth, had been president of Youth for Christ International, and I loved him as a dear friend. I figured if his son was anything at all like him, he would be quite a catch. Robert, along with Kip Jordon and Ernie Owen, was responsible for much of the publishing success at Word and was a very competent manager. I interviewed him and his wife Bobbi, at the Hyatt Hotel in Fort Worth, and later he came to Nashville.

Robert came with us, and we brought Michael Hyatt in shortly thereafter, president and vice president, respectively, of our Christian book division. They made a wonderful contribution bringing in books from such authors as Gary Smalley and Ron Blue. Meanwhile Vic Oliver had published outstanding books from authors like Gordon MacDonald and Charles Stanley. Soon the book division was vying with the Bible division for dollar-volume equality. Later Robert and Michael left to begin a new publishing company. It was a disappointment to me, but success doesn't usually come easily or quickly in this business.

Then Bruce Barbour joined Thomas Nelson to direct our book program, and we also hired Bob Zaloba to head sales. These men were very talented and by 1990, not only were we number one in Bible sales, but we were number one in Christian book sales. In fact, it was in that year that of the ten best-selling books in the Christian market in America, Thomas Nelson published five of them.

Chapter Twelve

All in the Family

As we continued to grow and expand—with new markets opening up, new products being developed, and some potential acquisitions in the wings—I found that my time was increasingly devoted to travel for the company. The downside for any of us with a growing business and a growing family is spending extended time away from home.

The Simple Life

Peggy and I had started out in a cozy old house on Watauga Avenue in Johnson City. It had a front porch, an eat-in kitchen, a living room, one bedroom, and a bath. Peggy was working at the time, and it was all we needed. After a couple of years, we moved to a bigger house on Oakland Avenue (the one that burned). We lived there until we moved to Nashville. Joe was born four years after we were married, and Peggy's mother took care of him while Peggy worked until we moved to Nashville.

In November 1965 Joe had turned three years old, and it

appeared he might be an only child. At the time of Peggy's surgery, the doctor had cautioned us that even though the surgery was successful and we had a child, she might not be able to conceive again. Peggy said to me one night over dinner, "You know how good God has been to us. If we want another child, perhaps we should check into adoption."

At that time many couples, because of local bureaucracy, were adopting children "behind the scenes." We felt strongly that if God wanted us to have a baby, He would open the door through our state adoption agency. While still in Johnson City we began our proceedings for adoption. Many people would say to us, "You're going to have to wait five years. They'll just drag their feet." When we moved to Nashville, our file was forwarded to the local agency.

While she was still working, Peggy and little Joe would often travel with me. She had worked long enough to have six weeks of annual leave. We would take long weekends, traveling to Nashville, Georgia, North Carolina, and South Carolina. Then for longer trips she used her vacation time. We could come and go as we pleased.

It seemed we were in and out of Nashville all the time. The Johnson City airport was rather small, and flight schedules were quite limited. To get to a final destination, I would have to make two or three stops. Nashville, being the capital and centralized in the state, had much easier access. Too, Nashville was a hub of printing and publishing with the Methodist and Southern Baptist operations there.

So the time came that for the best interests of all concerned, we should move to Nashville. It was very hard on Peggy to leave her hometown, her mother, and her job with the Social

Security Administration where she had worked for more than eleven years. She did look forward to simply staying at home and being a full-time wife and mother.

In 1965 we packed up and moved to Nashville to a rented house on Deerfield Drive in the Nashville suburb of Donelson. We lived there one year while we built our home in Mt. Juliet.

Mt. Juliet

We purchased some land, actually a farm, in the Nashville suburb of Mt. Juliet where we built our home. We moved there in April 1967. This is where our children were raised and where we lived happily for thirty-one years. Joe turned five that year.

Less than two years after filing, we got a call that a lovely little girl was up for adoption, and they wanted us to come and see her. We drove to the assigned meeting place and met for the first time this precious little girl who was already several weeks old. Immediately we fell in love with her. "Yes, we would love to have her," we told the lady in charge.

A short time later we were notified we had been selected as her parents. We named her Sandra Lee, and brought her to our home in October of 1967—her birthday was on June 18. By this time Joe was almost five. He was very proud of his baby sister. So here we were, a typical American family: mom and dad, a boy and a girl. We celebrated two big occasions that year—moving into a new home and welcoming a new daughter into the family.

As Joe grew, he developed a strong interest both in school and in athletics. Sandra, in her childhood years, related so well to younger children. Our hearts were touched as she would often help with the babies and young children during and after church.

There was a delightful couple, Odie and Lyda Adams, who lived on the Mt. Juliet property when we bought it. Odie had been born on the farm many years before, was injured in military service, and received a small retirement check each month from the government. But that wasn't enough to live on. I invited him to stay on in the small home they occupied, about two hundred yards from our place.

The hidden blessing for us was that for over twenty years Mr. and Mrs. Adams loved our children and often took care of them when Peggy and I were out of town on a business trip. They had no children of their own, so they treated our children as theirs. They were like another set of grandparents. These were special times for Joe and Sandra. In fact, sometimes on Saturday mornings when we were home, the kids would go down to their house, and Miss Lyda would fix them breakfast—biscuits from scratch, Uncle Odie's ham, grits, eggs, hotcakes—the whole works.

What happy years these were. We had a couple of ponds on the farm and often I'd get the kids up early in the morning to catch some fish.

Really, we lived quite worry-free as a family until the autumn of 1972, when Peggy began to complain of nausea and stomach pains. Naturally, we were concerned. You can imagine our shock when she visited the doctor and was told she was pregnant! After a decade of having no children naturally, we were expectant parents again. This was a joyous occasion for us.

Of course, Joe, being ten years old, wanted a boy since he already had a sister. Sandra, at six years old, wanted a sister since she already had a brother. For us, it didn't matter. We were thankful for a healthy baby. Dear Rachel Michelle came to join us on June 1, 1973. She has been a joy and blessing to us, especially after Joe and Sandra left home.

My father had passed away in 1972, and by the time Rachel came along, my mother had moved to Nashville to live. Peggy's mother was living next door to us on the farm. So our three children would have the joy of knowing both grandmothers.

Somber News

Enroute to our sales conference in Philadelphia in the fall of 1982, I stopped to call my sister in California where Mother was visiting. I was shocked to learn Mother had suffered a heart attack while walking through the Southcoast Plaza in Costa Mesa and had been rushed to the hospital. "She has taken a step for the worse," Mouna told me, "and she may not be here tomorrow."

I felt terrible. How could I go to address our salespeople when my mother was dying in southern California? I called Bernard Deeter and told him about the situation. He agreed to handle the sales conference, and I took the afternoon nonstop TWA flight from Philadelphia to Los Angeles.

With the time change, I got to L.A. in the early evening, and immediately rented a car and drove to University Hospital. Mother's face was an eerie blue color, and her hair seemed so very dull. Her eyes appeared glazed over, and I didn't think she was going to make it. I fell to my knees and asked God for mercy for her. "Would You just give her five years," I prayed, "so she can be with us and the children."

The next morning I woke up, dressed, and went back to the hospital to see Mama. Honestly, she was a different woman. Her hair was as white as snow, the color in her face had returned to a beautiful pink, and her eyes were sparkling. She squeezed my hand and said, "Son, I'm going to be okay."

I smiled and said, "You look real good, Mama. You look real good!"

The doctor walked in. "The worst is over, and we think she's going to be fine," he said. "But she will have to be careful."

They limit you to ten minutes in the critical care unit, but I managed to stay over half an hour before they ran me off. The medical staff was busy and evidently hadn't paid much attention to the time. I could come back that evening, so essentially I had the day to myself. People who know me realize I could not simply sit around, waiting for evening to come.

Tough Times Never Last, But Tough People Do!

For some time I had wanted to visit with Dr. Robert Schuller, who was known around the country for his television ministry. He had written several books, and I had been introduced to him a couple of times, but we had never had the chance to talk. I phoned his secretary, explained that I was in the area to visit with my stricken mother and that I had a few hours free to come see Dr. Schuller. Maybe he felt sorry for me, given my mother's condition, but at any rate he invited me to come by.

When I entered his office, I found him in his usual upbeat

manner, and he extended a warm welcome. My salesman's eye scanned his desk, and I noticed a manuscript sitting there.

"How is your mother?" he asked. "I would like to come and pray for her."

I told him I would like that very much. We talked about my mother's sudden heart attack while visiting in California, and how I had left our sales conference to come here to be at her side. I asked him about his family and ministry.

Then I said, "What is this manuscript on your desk?"

He said, "Oh, I have an agreement to send it to Doubleday, but I haven't signed the contract yet."

I urged him, "Don't sign it! Let me take it with me."

"Why should I let you take it?" he asked.

"Because I can make it a best-seller!" I told him. Robert Schuller is an optimist, but I don't think he was that optimistic.

"What makes you think you can turn it into a best-seller? I've had other publishers tell me that, and so far nothing much has happened." It turned out he had written some eighteen other books, and none made it to the best-seller list.

"I have a plan," I told him, "and if you will cooperate with me, we can make it a best-seller. We'll work together."

He told me what Doubleday was going to offer him for the book, and I said, "I will better their advance by $5,000." Now there was just silence in the room between us, and he was looking right at me. He seemed to be a bit irritated, and I thought I could see some doubt in his eyes. To close the sale, I needed to give him a reason to decide in favor of Thomas Nelson. A salesman is always selling himself, ultimately.

"Look," I asked him pointedly, "has the president of

Doubleday been here to see you? How about the head of Harper and Row? Has the chairman of Word ever come by personally and promised you that he could make your book a best-seller?"

Schuller looked totally surprised. He asked me why I was so sure I could pull it off.

"Because I own more of the company than anyone else does," I told him. "You're talking to the major shareholder. When I say I'll do something, you can count on it."

So we made a deal. We shook hands on it, and I took the manuscript with me.

By evening Mother was feeling even better, and the hospital was already talking about releasing her in a few days. My sister assured me she could handle Mama from then on. But I did ask my mother to promise me she would come back to Nashville as soon as she was ready to travel again.

Several days later I carried the Schuller manuscript back to Nashville and gave it to Larry Stone. He was scratching his head. "You paid too much money for this, Sam," he told me. But he was a smart editor, and he agreed to start working on it. Larry came up with a number of great ideas that could strengthen the manuscript in the editing phase, and Dr. Schuller worked with us as we readied his book for publication. And then we came up with the title, *Tough Times Never Last, But Tough People Do!*

We sold over 400,000 copies of the book in hardcover before it went into paperback, and Dr. Schuller personally visited over seventy-five bookstores in the process. By working together, we made it happen.

Within a few weeks, Dr. Schuller was visiting Hawaii and over lunch he was reading *Time* magazine. Lo and behold, on the best-seller list, according to both *The New York Times* and *Time* magazine, was his book. It had already made it to number three.

He called me from Hawaii, and he said, "Sam, you did it! You did it! You did it!"

I said, "I told you we would."

He said, "I'd like to celebrate by publishing another book with you."

We hurried up the editorial process on his second book, *Tough-Minded Faith for Tender-Hearted People,* and before we were through we had both of his books on the best-seller list simultaneously. It's rare that ever happens in publishing, and especially in Christian publishing, but I've got *The New York Times* best-seller clipping to prove it.

People asked me what we did to make Dr. Schuller a success. First of all, we did an outstanding editorial job on the book. Quality was important to us. Second, we made a decision to aggressively promote the book, and asked Dr. Schuller to promote it with us. He agreed to preach from the themes of the book for eight weeks on national television, holding it up before the camera. He took a tour to sign books, and we put ads in the papers in the towns where he appeared. People flocked in to see him at the various autograph sessions, and the book became an instant best-seller. In short, it was author-publisher teamwork.

You may recall that the mid- to late-1970s were a tough time economically in America. There was a shortage of gasoline, and many farmers were going broke because they could not afford to pay the taxes on their land. Dr. Schuller addressed the Farm Bureau in Chicago about the time his first book with us was coming out, and he told a story.

In his own youth a tornado came through Iowa and devastated their farmhouse, killed the horses, ruined everything. He explained how his family survived the hardship and rebuilt from scratch. He held up the book and told them, "You guys can do it too. When you commit your life to Christ there is a promise for you: Tough times never last, but tough people do." He had hit the nail right on the head, and the publicity people knew what to do with it.

As committed as I am to my business, as a Christian I've got to put principle ahead of the bottom line. As much as I felt I needed to talk with our salespeople in Philadelphia that day, there was another meeting more important: the one at the bedside of my mother.

I have learned over and over again that when I put the spiritual responsibilities in life ahead of the world of business and commerce, God will be there with an extra blessing. Not only did I experience the miraculous return of my mother to health, but as an aside there was a wonderfully successful new Thomas Nelson author in Dr. Robert Schuller. I had honestly never expected to talk personally with Dr. Schuller. I was in southern California for one reason, and ended up with both a healthy mother and two best-selling books.

Back on the Farm

Before long, Mother was back home with us in Nashville surrounded by three happy grandchildren. Life seemed always too busy for us, and I'm sure we endure many of the same stresses that any family faces. Raising three children in the world of the 1970s and the 1980s was never easy, and certainly we had our share of problems.

All around us we had friends and acquaintances who were calling it quits after ten or twenty years of marriage. We were living in a throwaway society. You could go to McDonald's, do the takeout, and throw away the plates and cups. Now they have even developed throwaway cameras. It goes without saying that this same era brought about the throwaway marriage.

I'd be a liar if I didn't say there were times I was tempted to walk out. I know I am constructed with a short fuse. Kids get sick, parents get frustrated, and problems seem to mount at home. Looking back after nearly forty years of marriage, there were things Peggy and I learned together that I feel a strong degree of confidence in passing on.

First of all, I grew up to believe that marriage is a sacrament, a sacred relationship. In reality, marriage happens in heaven as well as on earth. The first miracle Jesus ever performed was at a wedding, which means that marriage is set apart unto God with His blessing. The bed is pure and undefiled.

My mother and father always taught me marriage is for life. And if difficulties arise you have to work out the problems. You just don't bail out of the sacred union that God has given you. You take your hand off the back doorknob.

Second, in marriage I commit myself to my wife, and I must honor that commitment. No matter what. We say that we take each other for better or for worse. The problem today is that most people only want the better part and head out should the better get worse. Even in tough times, I don't deserve the wonderful wife I have. Thank God for Peggy. She is a far greater woman than I am a man. Four decades ago I told her it was for keeps, and I really meant it.

Third, we both realize the only way we can make this work is through our relationship with Jesus Christ. When He is the Lord and Master of our lives, He will give us the strength and resolve we need to work out whatever difficulties we have. And when we follow His will, our bond becomes even stronger.

In Ephesians 5, God calls us men to love our wives as Christ loves the church. The truth is, He loved His church enough to die for it. This means I have to be willing to suffer through the difficult times, that I must love her more than life itself. When a man makes that sort of promise to God and to his wife, and lives it out, there are few women who will yearn for something else.

Men, honestly, I think it's up to us. If we will love the Lord with all our heart, soul, mind, and strength, and pass on the love of Jesus Christ to our wives, I think we will be in our marriages for keeps. God's love and mercy have certainly worked wonderously for us in that respect.

Chapter Thirteen

The Acquisition Era

By 1982 Thomas Nelson had been the leading Bible publisher in the world for seven years. Furthermore, the evangelical book program was well under way, and our titles were gaining more and more prominence in Christian and even secular bookstores. The New King James Version of the Bible was penetrating virtually all markets, gaining broad support from Christian leaders across the spectrum. With our internal growth momentum so well established, I felt it was time to bring some new companies into the Thomas Nelson family.

But acquiring other companies is rarely a sure thing. With so many complications, so many pluses and minuses in the acquisition arena, it simply does not work every time.

A CEO has to be careful when acquiring a business to not just be enamored by the volume of sales that the firm has shown in the past. There are several other questions you must answer as well. How does the new company fit your present business? Where will you take the new acquisition after you purchase it? And how do the managers and owners (or shareholders) get along with one another in that company? If they are in conflict, you must find that out before you close the deal, or you may be paying dearly for other people's problems. Trust me. I know!

Dodd Mead

With our Christian book program aggressively moving ahead, we felt we needed to be more prominent in secular publishing. To do that, we would need to find a company that understood Thomas Nelson's identity as the major Bible publisher.

In 1982 we paid the Dodd Mead shareholders $1,800,000 for their company. Dodd Mead had specialized in reference books, sports books, a few children's series, and the famous Agatha Christie mysteries.

Before Dodd Mead was on board, we needed somebody to run it. I had known Lou Gillinson for some time and believed he was a great editor with a keen sense for books that would sell. Lou felt he could create books and acquire authors that would fit well with the Thomas Nelson philosophy. We wanted to expand into reference books and dictionaries, and, with Lou's background in companies such as Funk & Wagnall, we felt he could do the job for us. He owned a small company, Everest House, which we purchased. We consolidated it with Dodd Mead and made Lou president of that combined operation. Gloria Mosesson, who was our able and competent children's books editor, became part of Lou's team in New York City.

Lou did a fine job for us overall, pushing up revenues and publishing several important books. The difficulty came in combining the two cultures of our companies. At times we were at odds philosophically. We never interfered in Dodd Mead editorial policy, but we had insisted from the start that the book list of Dodd Mead could not bring any discredit to a company that was a major Bible publisher throughout the English-speaking world.

Interstate Book Manufacturing Company

Within a year of buying Dodd Mead, we purchased the Interstate Book Manufacturing Company located near Kansas City. In fact, one plant was in Kansas City, another about thirty miles outside of town in Olathe, Kansas. Our goal was to create a first-class plant and warehousing facility in the Midwest. Our major printer decided to get out of manufacturing. We felt we could do it ourselves. We expanded into a brand-new plant, 280,000 square feet under one roof with several new presses and two lines of binding, all of this giving us the capability of producing a number of our own Bibles and books.

This time our problems were economic. Ronald Reagan had become president in 1983 and instigated a new policy of less interference from government into the world of business. This opened the door for new imports. Meanwhile the English pound slipped down to the value of the dollar. This was the first time in my entire life I could remember the dollar being equal to the pound. While we were trying to build up the best book and Bible bindery in the world, books and Bibles were coming in from England and other European countries and were being sold in America for less than we could make them ourselves.

We had started feeding the plant new books and Bibles in order to keep the operation busy. What it did, however, was increase our cost of goods. Shelf space for our products was getting harder to find in the stores because the cost of our books was going higher. When we raised our prices to cover our costs, our overseas competitors moved in on us. We had to take decisive action. It would just be a matter of time before we would reverse our course, cut our losses, and sell the plant.

Ideals

It was also in 1983 that we purchased Ideals, famous for its children's books and annual Christmas magazine. This publication was a clean-cut, four-color, semi-inspirational magazine with beautiful pictures and text printed on glossy calendared stock. Content included poems, wonderful quotations, a biblical outlook on life, and it came with an incredibly loyal mailing list.

Management at Ideals was very sympathetic to our mission and philosophy at Thomas Nelson, and Pat Pingry, the editor in chief, came with a strong set of Christian values. We felt very much at home with Ideals, and I believe the feeling was mutual.

Morningstar

Morningstar was a fairly new Christian greeting card company out of Minneapolis. We believed the acquisition of this company would complement our book and Bible list at Thomas Nelson by getting us into thousands of new retail gift outlets. There was a competing company, called DaySpring, which carried a similar line of cards and was better established.

About this same time, DaySpring merged with David C.

Cook in Elgin, Illinois, which gave them enough cash to compete more effectively not only with us, but with the big boys such as American Greeting Cards and Hallmark. With our lack of expertise in the gift and greeting card business, we realized we may not be up for the battle.

A Time to Buy, a Time to Sell

By 1984 Thomas Nelson was as close to being on the verge of bankruptcy as we have ever been. We were accumulating huge losses, and our future was clouded at best. The dollar's slippage against the pound was the straw that broke the camel's back. We could not compete against overseas prices. We knew we had a white elephant on our hands with Interstate in Kansas City. We were losing money on this manufacturing operation, and it was time to put up the "FOR SALE" sign.

I thought back to what I had said years earlier to Lord Thompson, when I told him there would be a time in God's economy when all of us would have to sell. My words came back to haunt me!

Being competitive to the core, it has always been far easier for me to acquire than it has been to unload. Most managers know when it's a good time to buy; very few of us are detached enough from our businesses to know that it is a "must" time to sell. So we had to hunker down and eliminate the business that we did not know how to manage well: the actual printing and manufacturing of books.

We sold Interstate to W. A. Kruger for about what we paid for it. However, we had added a lot of expensive equipment, so the sale of the company was a loss item for us. This transaction was completed in 1987, following the sale of Dodd Mead in 1986.

That same year we also decided to sell Morningstar, which found a new home with Warner Press. Though we had done far better with Ideals, that company was sold in 1987 as well. We decided we had to go back to the publishing we knew best, books and Bibles.

By 1990 the Thomas Nelson company had returned to a very solid, very profitable position. Its lustre had been restored. We had ten wonderful quarters of consistent profit and the investment houses of America rediscovered us. Stock began selling at a good multiple again.

By the opening of the decade of the 1990s, there were three major publishing companies in the Christian market that were the leaders in book, Bible, and music publishing: Thomas Nelson, Zondervan, and Word. Zondervan was independent at the time and publicly held, but it later sold to Harper, which was a division of News Corp. Word was owned by Capital Cities ABC.

Editorial Caribe

In 1991 we decided to buy the Spanish publishing arm of the Latin American Mission, Editorial Caribe. Juan Rojas, the president of the organization, felt he could operate the mission better without the publishing responsibility. We bought Editorial Caribe at a reasonable price, expanded the operation and the office space, and started translating our own religious reference works and Bibles into Spanish.

A short time later we also added Editorial Betania and merged it with Caribe to become one company. After a few initial problems, this company has grown, and we feel that the future of Spanish religious publishing will be strong. We are keeping a close eye on this operation to be sure that overhead and expansion will not overcome the profit margin. Its offices are in Miami and Nashville.

Here's Life Publishers

Before the year 1991 came to a close we purchased Here's Life Publishers from Campus Crusade. For any organization or denomination to create and build their own publishing arm is a heavy burden to bear. It must be large enough to compete in both the secular and religious marketplace and because of government restrictions on the nonprofit status, this is often a challenge that is virtually impossible to meet. In acquiring Here's Life, we picked up a stable of outstanding authors and consolidated that operation into our company.

Word, Inc.

Our biggest and most successful acquisition to date came in 1992 when we bought our major competitor, Word, Inc., from Capital Cities ABC. Cap City didn't feel comfortable keeping this overtly religious music and publishing company, and several interested parties were bidding for it. They obtained the services of Goldman Sachs to sell it for them.

PaineWebber of New York City represented Thomas Nelson, and their team was made up of George Stephenson, Julian

Markby, and several other key PaineWebber people. George was our chief negotiator, and he was very conscientious. He thought their $90 million figure was too high and recommended we offer $70 million with the thought of going as high as $75 million to close the deal.

But we had a major contender in HarperCollins. That company was a powerhouse with sales of more than a half billion dollars, and they already owned Zondervan. This purchase would have been an ideal complement, adding value to their Zondervan acquisition. Jim Buick at Zondervan was pushing hard on behalf of HarperCollins, and they made an offer combining cash and securities. We came back with an offer of $70 million in cash, no securities involved, which was greater than the cash part of their offer. They rejected our offer, but since they were looking for the best cash deal they could find, we were still very definitely in the running.

We looked at Word one more time. I went and met with the management of the company: Roland Lundy, Byron Williamson, Kip Jordon, and Tom Stanton. I liked these managers and their evangelical Christian values and commitment. We decided to increase our offer to $72 million in exchange for a thirty-day exclusive right to purchase, during which time we could perform an intense procedure called "due diligence," Jim Cheeck our able attorney at Bass Berry & Sims called it "opening the kimono," in which a prospective buyer can learn absolutely everything there is to know about the company—a total disclosure of all financial records.

We had to produce a letter of credit from our bank confirming that Thomas Nelson could actually come up with the money if everything looked good. On Monday morning I called

In Religious Books, Preachers Top the Charts

Thomas Nelson and Word bestsellers dominate the list

BY WILLIAM GRIFFIN

Thomas Nelson with five titles and Word with four cleaned up in the 1991 hardcover religious bestsellers sweepstakes—Bibles excluded, of course. Add one each from Moody and Doubleday, and there are 11 frontlist religous titles that sold over 100,000 copies each last year.

While the books demonstrate considerable variety, with themes ranging from the inspirational to the international, what they have in common may be more telling in terms of their sales power. A key component of the marketing success for most of the books is undoubtedly the 'media ministries' of the authors. Benny Hinn, who has the #1 title, *Good Morning, Holy Spirit*, and a 7000-member church in Florida, runs a national cable show that is broadcast three times a day. Former presidential candidate Pat Robertson (#2) is longtime host of *The 700 Club*, which is broadcast in over 80 countries. Sales for those two titles were over 400,000 copies each. Crystal Cathedral founder Robert Schuller (*Life's Not Fair, But God is Good*; #3) preaches weekly on *The Hour of Power*, a widely watched televised church services. Christian radio listeners can hear Charles Swindoll (*Simple Faith*; #6) weekly on *Insights for Living*. Internationally known crusader Billy Graham (*Hope for the Troubled Heart*; #7) is a Christian radio regular. And Larry Burkett (*The Coming Economic Earthquake*; #5), president of a ministry dedicated to teaching God's principles for financial management, does daily radio shows.

Meanwhile, all but one of the remaining books on the list have built-in constituencies: *Little House in the Ozarks* (#8) would seem to be a must-buy for *Little House on the Prairie* fans past and present. Zig Ziglar (*Ziglar on Selling*; #9) has

been a sales and promotions professional for 40 years and has a long backlist of books and tapes. *Love Hunger: Recovery From Food Codependency* (#4) from Nelson's Minirth-Meier clinic is suggested reading for many eating disorder recovery groups.

PW's 1991 Religious Bestsellers

1. **Good Morning, Holy Spirit,** by Benny Hinn. Nelson; 438,241

2. **The New World Order** by Pat Robertson. Word; 407,189

3. **Life's Not Fair, But God Is Good** by Robert Schuller. Nelson; 188,750

4. **Love Hunger: Recovery From Food Codependency** by Frank Minirth, Paul Meier, Robert Hemfelt and Sharon Sneed. Nelson; 188,030

5. **The Coming Economic Earthquake** by Larry Burkett. Moody; 165,946

6. **Simple Faith** by Charles Swindoll. Word; 130,303

7. **Hope for the Troubled Heart** by Billy Graham. Word; 127,914

8. **Little House in the Ozarks: A Laura Ingalls Wilder Sampler—The Rediscovered Writings,** edited by Stephen Hines. Nelson; 123,000

9. **Ziglar on Selling: The Ultimate Handbook for the Complete Sales Professional** by Zig Ziglar. Nelson; 114,221

10. **In the Eye of the Storm** by Max Lucado. Word; 113,693

*11. **God, Country, Notre Dame** by Theodore M. Hesburgh with Jerry Reedy. Doubleday.

* Sales figures were submitted to *PW* in confidence, for use only in placing the title in its correct position on the list.

Alumni support for their alma mater's former 35-year president must contribute to the high sales of the #11 title, Theodore Hesburgh's *God, Country, and Notre Dame*. Since he retired in 1987, Hesburgh has been involved in activities relating to world peace, the environment, ecumenism and international development; these constituencies, too, provide buyers for his autobiography.

Only San Antonio preacher Max Lucado seems without an obviously large following for his sixth book, *In the Eye of the Storm*, which is about the only day in the life of Jesus that was recorded by all four evangelists. Comments Word publisher Kip Jordon, "Lucado's books travel on the printed page alone."

Successful crossover into the secular marketplace also contributes to the high sales figures for the Christian titles. Both Jordon and Hugh Barbour, Thomas Nelson's publisher, estimate that 50% of sales for their '91 bestsellers in general trade stores. *Good Morning, Holy Spirit* spent nine months on *PW*'s hardcover religious bestseller list, which was begun in February 1991 and takes its data from general independent stores, major chains, and wholesalers. *The New World Order* and *Life's Not Fair, but God is Good* both went on the list last fall and are still there as of March. Clearly these titles are selling in CBA and non-CBA stores alike.

Comments Barbour: "Our competition is Random House and Simon & Schuster—that's the shelf space I'm fighting for in the Waldens and Daltons." Barbour says he thinks the expectations for marketing plans, packaging, and editorial content are "frankly, I believe, much higher" in the general retail market than in the religious trade. □

Bob Dudiak, our man at SunTrust Bank in Atlanta, and
need $72 million, and I need it by Friday."

He and Fred Turner, at SunTrust in Nashville, were
surprised. "Golly, you didn't give us any warning," the
"And you've never asked for that much before."

They were right. The most we'd borrowed before wa
or $30 million, and now we were asking for $72 millio
wanted to bet the farm with it. But by Friday morning wi
help of John Clay Jr., President of the bank in Nashville, w
our letter of credit, ensuring our ability to make the purc

I immediately sent about a half dozen certified publi
countants and key managers along with two or three othe
countants from Arthur Anderson to examine the books at W
checking all the liabilities, reviewing all the intangibles,
determining the future of the business. Cap Cities had over
million in Word, and after all disclosure was complete, we
cided the company was a good buy at $72 million.

Overall, Word was about the same size as Thomas Nel
It was composed basically of two businesses: 48 percent l
publishing and 52 percent music. Why did we want the c
pany? Part of what attracted our attention was that in 1
according to *Publishers Weekly* magazine, Thomas Nelson
five of the best-selling books and Word had four among th
ten of the religious and inspirational titles in America.

Because Word was a leader in the Christian music bus
this would mean that Thomas Nelson would be the pr
publisher of Christian books, Bibles, and Christian
among all its competitors. This, for me, would be an
dream come true.

When we bought Word, the president was Roland L

Roland is a very fine Christian with great talent for working with people and managing a company. Roland ran the music end at Word; Byron Williamson, a competent and capable executive, ran the book program. Roland and I both knew that for Word to grow, some significant changes needed to be made. I think Cap Cities ABC knew that as well.

At Word most of the creative work in the music division was done in Nashville while the management was in Dallas. Although it was tough on Roland and his family to move, Roland knew he had to be on top of the music. We consolidated all of the music in Nashville and Roland moved there to take charge of that operation. We segmented the book publishing from the music and put books under Word executive Byron Williamson. The fruit of Roland's labor is obvious. By early 1997 the music group at Nelson was doing about $100 million a year, which was about 30 percent of our company's business.

Let me say that music is a very different animal from book publishing, both because of the direct marketing music clubs and also because of its international scope and unpredictability. In music, you are dealing with artists and you are depending on "hits." If you produce hits, you make it big. If you don't, you don't. Management hates it when income is irregular, but that is simply part of the music business.

Word book publishing, as I said, was consolidated under Byron Williamson, a capable executive with a great nose for good books. His editor in chief was the late Kip Jordon, one of the finest publishers I have met anywhere—a bright man who knows how to handle authors and get the best from them. The Word team, which included Joey Paul, David Moberg and Lee Gessner, built a list of authors that dominated the industry.

Max Lucado, James Dobson, Charles Swindoll, Billy Graham, Barbara Johnson, Pat Robertson, and Charles Colson—and that's just the short list.

Byron added numerous skills to our publishing and management. We have consolidated all of our publishing companies under his leadership. Each of the publishers report to him. We also created several categories of book products. Nelson and Word, as well as our children's book division, Tommy Nelson and our gift book division, Countryman, will, however, be maintained as distinct publishing programs. Most of the bookstore people would prefer to place one order rather than two. Jerry Park is a most gifted motivator, the man heading up our combined sales operation in the CBA (Christian Booksellers Association) area. Ron Land, one of the ablest marketing men in the industry who left Word a few years back and later came to Nelson, heads the mass-merchandizing and general trade market sales.

The Gift Division

Though the Thomas Nelson gift division is not an acquisition in any sense of the word, I want to say something about it here because it fits in so well chronologically to our acquisition era. The other reason I want to say something about it is because it is run by my son, Joe.

Joe had started selling books door-to-door for our Varsity division in the summer of 1981 after he finished high school. I remember telling Peggy, "He'll be back home within two weeks."

Peggy didn't like that. "You don't have faith in your own son," she told me.

I said, "Honey, it's not that I don't have faith in him. I just don't think he wants to be a salesman. Sales is not his thing."

How is it that we men think we know our own sons so well? Joe became Varsity's number one salesman that year. He saved $9,800 after expenses. That's just for ten weeks' work! I couldn't believe my own son could do that well and be number one out of three hundred in the first-year sales force.

The second year he became number one again, as he did the third and fourth years. That fourth year, while he was a senior at Vanderbilt, he actually saved about $25,000 after expenses. To celebrate, after his graduation I took him on a European vacation for thirty days, just father and son, and we had the best time of our lives. Besides praying together every night and reading the Bible, we visited France, England, Italy, and Germany. In Paris we stayed at the home of our United States Ambassador to France, Joe Rodgers and his lovely wife, Honey.

It was tempting for me to offer my son a job right out of college, but I think he and I both felt that it would be best for him to cut his eyeteeth somewhere else for a while. He started out as an advertising salesman at a television station in Baltimore and worked his way up to sales manager and later to assistant manager for the entire operation. While in Baltimore, Joe enrolled at the University of Maryland in their MBA program. He made straight As and finished summa cum laude with a 3.9 average.

By the time Joe came back to Nashville, he not only had his MBA degree but he had become a wizard in computers and knew finances.

Traditionally, about 80 percent of our business had come from our Bible division. Joe said, "If you have all the Bible business in the world, you aren't going to grow the company. Dad, you're publicly held, and you need to grow. That means you need to diversify."

"You smart aleck," I shot back at him, "why don't you start helping us diversify. Let's see how good you are."

"You should diversify in the gift area," Joe advised me. I asked Bernard Deeter to help Joe for the first year to get him organized in the book trade. We took the paintings and the color illustrations from our Precious Moments Bible and created gift items from the artwork. Joe called this company Markings.

That first year Joe brought in $700,000 from his division and the second year $1,800,000. By the third year his division garnered $2,900,000, which grew to $6,000,000 in the fourth year, and then nearly $10,000,000 in the fifth year. At that point he bought another company called Pretty Paper, which had been a major competitor of ours. Within seven years, the gift division of Thomas Nelson was doing $26,000,000 a year under Joe's leadership.

In 1995 another of our competitors, the C. R. Gibson Company, which was listed on the American Stock Exchange, came up for sale. Their business history included greeting cards, baby gifts, photo albums, and other gift-related items. We paid $64,000,000 for the company, which has brought us into some tremendously expanded markets. As we celebrate the two-hundredth anniversary of the Thomas Nelson company, the gift division has grown tremendously.

In January of 1997 we completed the sale of our Word Records and Music division to Gaylord Entertainment Company for $110 million. This was another win-win situation because we wanted to focus more on our traditional businesses and Gaylord wanted to further expand into an area where they were already a leader with their ownership of Z Music Television, The Ryman Auditorium, and the Grand Ole Opry.

Finally, the acquisition era worked. The company is more stable in its diversification than it has ever been.

Change Is the Only Constant

We created the Royal Media group in 1994 to pursue broadcasting and new media opportunities. We hired Rolf Zettersten from Focus on the Family to run this new division. In the ensuing year there were unsettling changes in the cable and multimedia industries. Cap Cities ABC was sold to Disney, Turner was sold to Time Warner, and CBS was sold to Westinghouse. We decided to wait until things settled and the technology was more clearly defined. Rolf Zettersten accepted a new assignment to head Nelson's publishing division. He has ink in his blood, and is doing an outstanding job working with such fine Thomas Nelson authors as Dr. Charles Stanley, John C. Maxwell, Brock and Bodie Thoene, Franklin Graham, and Cynthia Heald.

Despite the ups and downs of the acquisition era, we as a company still came out ahead! In fact, we kept over $120 million in sales acquisition assets after all was said and done, and realized over $75 million in profits for our shareholders. But so far, I'm still waiting on the business editors of our American newspapers and magazines to report that facet of the story.

Chapter Fourteen

Some Thoughts
on Leadership

I believe no one has a corner on the market of success. The world is full of many enterprising men and women who are far more successful than I have ever been or would dream to be. Many of them have written bestselling books and inspiring articles setting forth their leadership and success principles. So let me simply summarize six principles of leadership that have guided me in my work over the years.

Vision

For me, the first principle of leadership is vision. No leader can simply "accomplish things" in a vacuum. Effective leadership requires a vision. In the Old Testament, God gave Abraham a vision and asked him to leave his home and go to a new country. God gave Nehemiah a vision to build a wall.

Most outstanding business ventures today begin with a vision. Tom Watson had a vision to automate technology and he created one of the giant industries of our time, IBM. Sam

Walton had a vision to sell quality products at the lowest possible prices, and Wal-Mart was born in Bentonville, Arkansas. At first, by the way, people scoffed and laughed at him. Today Wal-Mart does over $100 billion in revenue. Not many people laugh at Sam Walton's ideas now!

Kip Jordon had a vision to create Christian books for the broader Christian community instead of focusing just on his denomination. He accepted a job with Word as their editor. Today the fruit of his vision shows, and he published some of the best Christian authors in America. Max Lucado is a wonderful author Kip developed.

At the CBA convention in Chicago in the early 1960s, I met with Ken Taylor, an editor at Moody Press. He had written a Bible study book for kids called *Bible Stories for Little Eyes*. I was inspired that its simple message held the attention of young children. I told him, "It would be good if you could do the whole Bible in that form."

He began with the Epistles, the writings of Paul the apostle, and then added the rest. Later he finished the Gospels and called it *The Living New Testament*.

I told him, "Ken, you should do the whole Bible."

He said, "The Lord hasn't told me to do the whole Bible, Sam."

I said, "I believe the Lord told me that you should finish the whole Bible!"

The Living Bible became an enlightenment to millions of people around the world. I thank God for Ken Taylor.

During that same CBA convention years ago, Ken and another friend, Harold Shaw, came to my room. We knelt and prayed about my going into business on my own and going public with the stock. I had a vision of creating easy-to-under-stand Bibles and books for the Christian community. These two godly men laid hands on me, and asked God to bless this vision. This book is the story of how the Lord answered our prayers and brought the vision to reality.

In Proverbs 29:18, God says, "Where there is no vision, the people perish" (KJV). A church without a vision will soon atrophy. A company without a visionary leader will drift in confusion and disorder. Mahatma Gandhi envisioned an India free from British rule. Henry Ford had a vision that every American family would be able to afford an automobile.

A leader is one who believes his vision and transfers that vision to his management. The management group becomes committed to follow their leader in the vision, and this becomes the mission of their company. A united corporate leadership becomes the feet that carry that vision, the engine that drives the vision to fulfillment.

Merely having a vision is not enough. You join it to a mutual commitment to orchestrate the vision into a mission.

Faith

The second principle of success is faith. For the Christian, God gives the vision, but the leader must have faith in God that the vision will be accomplished. The book of Hebrews teaches that "without faith it is impossible to please Him" (11:6 NKJV).

I remember the first time I heard Chuck Swindoll preach in Fullerton, California. Every time I heard him I became enthused, and I felt he should be telling his story to America. Clarence Hagman, our Thomas Nelson salesman in California, was a member of Swindoll's congregation. Clarence felt the same way.

When I asked Charles Swindoll about writing a book early in the 1970s, he didn't feel he could commit himself to such a project. Later I asked our editor, Peter Gillquist, to go see him. They had gone to seminary together. Peter called me after the visit. "Sam, Chuck Swindoll hasn't written anything and says he doesn't want to write."

My answer to Peter was, "Don't come back until you find material for a book by Swindoll. A speaker that good has the potential to be a great writer." My faith wouldn't let me take no for an answer.

Peter came back to the office and told me, "Chuck has a set of twelve live messages on tape called 'You and Your Child.' This could be transformed into a book, but it's going to take a lot of work."

That was the first of three books we published by Chuck Swindoll. Several years later Swindoll started working with Word Publishing. He has written numerous outstanding books. One of his best, in my opinion, is *The Grace Awakening*. It is probably one of the best books ever written on living by faith and letting God's grace abound in you.

I wonder sometimes what happened to simple Christian faith, the childlike faith of trusting Jesus Christ. When you have Christ-reliant faith, you have peace within your soul, your inner being. You are relaxed, contented, and joyful in your life—even if it flows at a maddening pace.

The Bible says, "Ask in prayer, believing" (Matt. 21:22 NKJV). Faith is simply the assurance that God will answer our prayers, will be with us, and help us cross oceans, rivers, and mountains. Can you imagine the fear I had at nineteen when I left the old country to come by myself to learn a new language? I had faith that God would be with me as I met new people, experienced new customs in a new way of life. He has been so faithful to me.

Goal Setting

Once my vision is clear and my faith is in place, it's time to set some goals. For a vision to be fulfilled it must have specific goals, and these goals must be both achievable and measurable.

There is a difference between a goal and a purpose. A purpose is something for which we ultimately hope (like publishing understandable Christian literature), but a purpose is not necessarily measurable. What purpose does provide is clear direction. There are many organizations that state their purpose but lack a definition of this purpose or a plan for accomplishing it.

Your goal is ultimately the way to accomplish your purpose. Alan Mathis, former president of American Management Association, used to say to me, "If it is not measurable it is not doable." So goals not only must be measurable but also practical and achievable. No leader can rise and excel without a vision and the goals to accomplish it.

There are four basic reasons people are often afraid to set goals.

1. *Laziness.* **It is difficult to put forth the extra effort of creatively thinking through the goals that must be set and writing them out.**

2.   *Fear of failure.* Babe Ruth was the greatest hitter of all time. However, as many have observed, he had more strikeouts than most other baseball players of his time.

3.   *Lack of discipline.* People are not willing to discipline themselves and change the status quo.

4.   *Fear of ridicule.* People worry that bad things may happen and they'll be criticized for it. Often the bad things never happen at all. However, in the midst of their worry they are defeated.[1]

What good does goalsetting do for an organization? It gives the company the power to live in the present. A book compiled by Robert C. Larson, *The Best of Ted Engstrom on Personal Excellence and Leadership*, reveals the power of goals: A sense of direction and purpose allowing people to see where their gifts and abilities are best utilized within the company structure.

When people know they are working together for the common good of the company, there is an increased sense of teamwork. It is much easier to build trust around a task that people are accomplishing together.

Goals help us evaluate our progress and increase our effectiveness. Goals help us to communicate within the organization; people know who does what and who is responsible for what. Goals give people a clear understanding of what is expected. Finally, goals take the emphasis off activity and place it on results.

You have already seen the incredible role that goalsetting has played here at Thomas Nelson. When I started in the business, my first goal, my short-range goal, was to be the best Bible publisher in the world. That goal was set in the late 1960s. When I acquired Thomas Nelson, I was able to accomplish that short-range goal.

My long-range goal was to be the leader in the Christian bookstore arena in the three categories of Bibles, books, and gifts or music. Thomas Nelson had a sales record in 1969 of $1,442,000. Among the ten outstanding publishers at the time we were number ten. My goal was to be number one in ten years. We reached the goal in 1976. Thomas Nelson was not only number one, we were bigger than numbers two and three combined. My second goal was dependent on the first short-range goal being accomplished.

The overall guide for goal setting is:

1. **Do not make too many short-range goals. Limit goals to a few major objectives.**
2. **Assign goals to people and then hold them accountable.**
3. **People must grow to share your vision and goals.**
4. **You must help your team to achieve that goal.**[2]

One last thing. No goal is easily attainable. There will always be problems along the way. F. F. Fournies outlines four common reasons why people do not perform the way they should:

1. **They do not know *what* they are supposed to do.**
2. **They do not know *how* to do it.**
3. **They do not know *why* they should do it.**
4. **There are obstacles beyond their control.**[3]

We all encounter problems. According to John Maxwell, the size of the person is more important than the size of the problem. A manager or leader needs to help his people solve the problem. When you help solve the problem, you create confidence and you begin to reach the goal.

Discipline

Once you set the goal, it takes a fierce discipline to reach it. Discipline can be categorized into three areas: (1) individual discipline or self-discipline; (2) team discipline; (3) market discipline.

Besides Zig Ziglar, John Maxwell is probably the best motivational and leadership seminar speaker in America. He is also a best-selling author for Thomas Nelson and one of my heroes. He consistently brings in fresh ideas on numerous subjects, and he excels in the area of self-discipline. Regarding individual discipline he says in his book *Developing the Leader Within You,* "We cannot travel without until we first travel within. When we are foolish, we want to conquer the world. When we are wise we want to conquer ourselves. I am my biggest enemy. I have to learn how to conquer me."

In *The Discipline of Market Leaders* by Michael Treacy and Fred Wiersma, the authors say,

> The market leaders today excel by delivering one type of value to their chosen customers. The key, of course, in today's market is focus. Market leaders choose a single value discipline—best total cost, best product, or best total solution—and then build their

organization around it. They sustain their leadership position not by resting on their laurels, but by offering better value year after year.[4]

Major corporations today are changing their emphasis to satisfy the customer. Organizations like Charles Schwab and AT&T conduct business at times most convenient to their customers, not just to themselves.

The new world of competition is tough. Companies can no longer just raise prices. Companies can no longer aim for less than hassle-free service. Customers are demanding effortless, flawless performance. We can no longer assume that good basic service is enough. People are demanding premium service. Market discipline means we cannot compromise on quality and product capability. We must build our products to deliver nothing less than superiority and eye-popping innovation. In other words, "the customer is king."

In their book, Wiersma and Traecy tell us there are three major disciplines a company can concentrate on:

1. *Operational excellence.* **This is Wal-Mart, the company which delivers the best quality product for the lowest price with the least hassle.**
2. *Product leadership.* **A company like Nike delivers quality athletic footwear for outstanding performers.**
3. *Customer intimacy.* **That's where the company gets to know its customers and delivers products the customer absolutely must have. For that, the customer is willing to pay what those premium services cost. The model is Airborne Express.[5]**

In today's environment, where the world is changing so fast and the competition is so keen, the market is demanding far better service than five or ten years ago. Disciplined market leaders understand they have to focus better, they need to understand their customers better, and deliver a product hassle-free. In short, they have specific goals and meet them.

Time Management

In business and management schools we hear about the Pareto Principle, the 80/20 rule. You prioritize your work in order to spend 20 percent of your time on the things that produce 80 percent of the results. In our company, 20 percent of our books produce 80 percent of the sales. We therefore spend the best of our time developing and selling these books.

Time is the only equal opportunity commodity. Some people are more intelligent than others, some have more money and resources, some have more talents—but everybody has the same amount of time each twenty-four-hour day. Effective leaders manage their time to the max. Often it is time management that makes the difference between an outstanding leader and an average leader.

Peter Drucker writes, "Effective executives . . . do not start with their tasks. They start with their time. And they do not start out with planning. They start by finding out where their time actually goes."[6]

Stephanie Winston, in her book *Best Organizing Tips,* says, "There are two simple rules for the busiest people and for effective executives: (1) figure what is most important, (2) create your own time plan." In order to prioritize time, she believes we need two lists of "to dos." One list she calls the master list; the other one is the daily list.[7]

I have been using her "two lists" plan for some time. It works! I keep the master list at my house, and I have two or three index cards for daily tasks in my pocket or notebook. Continually, I am jotting things down I have to do. Later, I incorporate these notes into my master list.

For example, there are tax forms I must return by a certain date. Or home football games I want to attend. Or business trips I have to make. I have all these on my master list. (I also put them in my calendar so my secretary will have record of them.)

I try to break my tasks down into manageable parcels to avoid being overwhelmed. Each day I check my master list for the things I need to do. I cross off what has been done. At the end of every day I add items to the master list that I have gathered from my pocket notes during that day.

I know some people who use index cards for their master list. There are others who use handheld organizers or their computers. Any of these items will work.

On my daily list I organize the items according to their priority. Sometimes unexpected things happen. These things go on my daily list as well. Of first priority is the list of items that I absolutely must do. I mentioned earlier the Pareto Principle. Those things that bring 80 percent of my results need as much of my time as possible. They are priority!

Low importance, low urgency matters, such as the busy or repetitious work of filing, need to be delegated. Key leaders and effective people have to realize they can't do everything.

Sometimes you have to choose between two good things. My father said to me a long time ago, "The good is often the greatest enemy of the best!" Choose to do the things that are important to the fulfillment of your goals.

Don't list too many priorities. This will bring confusion, and you will accomplish none of them. A sacred rule is "Keep it simple." If you don't prioritize, you fail. The sooner you prioritize the better.

Attitude

Chuck Swindoll, in *Improving Your Serve,* says this about attitude:

> The longer I live, the more I realize the impact of attitude on life. Attitude, to me, is more important than facts. It is more important than the past, than education, than money, than circumstances, than failure, than successes, than what other people think or say or do. It is more important than appearance, giftedness, or skill. It will make or break a company, a church, or a home.

> The remarkable thing is that we have a choice every day regarding the attitude we will embrace for that day. We cannot change our past. Nor can we change the fact that people will act in a certain way. We also cannot change the inevitable. The only thing that we can do is play on the one string we have, and that is our attitude. I am convinced that life is 10 percent what happens to me and 90 percent how I react to it. And so it is with you—we are in charge of our attitude.[8]

Lou Holtz, former Notre Dame football coach, says, "Ability is what you are capable of doing, motivation determines what you do, attitude determines how well you do it."

If attitude is so important, what causes a bad attitude, and how can we correct it? I'm sure different things get to different people. But for me, setbacks and failures are the great progenitors of bad attitude. For you it might be a D on a report card, losing the first three games of the season, a canceled contract, a 250-point dip in the stock market.

I've told you about Blue Monday, our printing debacle in Kansas City, and our initial failure with the greeting card business. Honestly, things like this are an attitude killer for me. Three times in my life since becoming the leader in the religious publishing industry, I have had a lousy attitude.

The worst was the day in 1995 when we released an earnings report that failed Wall Street expectations by a large margin. I had gone to bed the night before with TNM at over 25. By morning it had dropped to 15. Bah! It only takes one day of setback to give you the feeling of unwantedness. I feel sorry for my employees who had to look at my long face in the days and weeks that followed that event.

I am quite optimistic by nature, but this 1995 setback seemed to overshadow all other past success. I had enjoyed four decades of financial blessings with only three setbacks. But at my age, this was the hardest setback I ever had to face. I thought that in my mid-sixties, these emotional droops were behind me. On top of everything else, I was in the process of building a new house, and it was taking three times as long as it was supposed to with huge cost overruns. Those who report to me and other staff would have preferred that I just stay home, I'm sure. I knew I had to change my attitude.

I thank God that time has passed and things have improved. Some of the best men I know—Jack Massey, Andrew Young, Carl Young—have all had major setbacks. Those who know how to rebound and come back are the ones who succeed in life.

Let me speak plainly. People with a bad attitude usually end up losers. A positive attitude usually winds up winning. By nature, some people tend to have a bad attitude. It may be stimulated by their backgrounds, their families, their failures, their upbringing. They often turn out to be losers. It is very hard to help them to change their attitudes. May I offer some help?

First, we are responsible for our attitude. People say, "Well, I inherited my negative attitude from my parents." Maybe that's true. But you can correct your attitude! You can take control of your attitude.

Jesus said, "Come to Me, all you who labor and are heavy laden, and I will give you rest" (Matt. 11:28 NKJV). Victor Frankl once asserted, "The last of the human freedoms is to choose one's attitude in any given set of circumstances." Positive attitude comes from within. God can give you the power to change. Believe that you can succeed, and try again when you fail. But you have to believe that God will change you.

Second, the attitudes of leaders affect their followers. I'm learning that during those times of crisis in my life, I can do a lot of good just by being positive toward the people around me. We are fortunate to have Ray Capp on our Nelson team, because he always has a good attitude. His manner is infectious, and that blesses the whole company.

Third, here on earth there is no one with the ability to unceasingly maintain a perfect attitude. No one feels good all the time. We are affected by the circumstances of our lives. Someone might ask me how I'm doing. My answer could be, "Well, under the circumstances, not so bad." But wait—what am I doing under the circumstances? I'm supposed to be on top of the circumstances!

Finally, we must be willing to change our attitude. We cannot wallow in self-pity and dismay. We must let it go.

A man I have greatly admired over the years is a fellow immigrant, the late Robert Goizuetta, a Cuban refugee who went on to become head of Coca-Cola™. Though enormously successful, he also brought us one of the great marketing debacles of the 20th century, "New Coke." His attitude toward his mistakes? "You can't stumble if you're not moving. And if you stumble and make a decision that doesn't pan out, then you move quickly to change it. But it's better than standing still."[9]

Ask yourself, "What do I have to do to change?" If you have had a setback, then commit to succeed where you formerly failed. But to do so will require that you first change your attitude. You'll have to believe you can succeed, and take the word *quit* out of your vocabulary.

Many of us believe after we fail that failure is final. Failure is never final as long as you keep trying. Football game films show consistently that in the NFL, 85 percent of the tackles are made by guys who were taken out of the play. But they get back up to stop the runner.

In Romans 12:1–2, Paul writes, "I beseech you therefore, brethren, by the mercies of God, that you present your bodies a living sacrifice, holy, acceptable to God, which is your reasonable service. And do not be conformed to this world, but be transformed by *the renewing of your mind*, that you may prove what is that good and acceptable and perfect will of God" (NKJV, italics mine).

In Psalm 37:4 we read, "Delight yourself also in the LORD, and He shall give you the desires of your heart" (NKJV). If you trust in God, He can change your thoughts and fulfill your desires.

After a setback a person has to make significant changes. You may have to develop a whole new set of good habits—one of life's most challenging tasks. I promise you will not find this easy or immediate. Bad thoughts, negative attitudes, wrong decisions, wrong actions—these all lead to failure. However, right thoughts, positive outlook, right decisions, and right actions create good attitudes and lead to success.

There are two keys that determine who we are: Who we conceive ourselves to be, and who we associate with. Develop positive supporting friends. Commit to at least one person you can talk to, heart to heart and soul to soul. Do this with much prayer and careful consideration. Make sure this person is worthy of your trust. Your pastor might be a good place to start. If that person is a real friend, he will stand with you in good times and in bad times.

In his book *And the Angels Were Silent*, Max Lucado observes, "A man who wants to lead the orchestra must turn his back on the crowd."

Progress Is a Process

The older I get, the more clearly I see that leadership is a growth process. A magic wand will not work. You have major turning points in your life, as I've had in mine, and things will improve dramatically. But there will still be more to learn, or maybe relearn.

There is great satisfaction in improvement and victory. It is my prayer that both the successes and the setbacks of my career will help provide you with a road map by which you may better chart your course.

Chapter Fifteen

Thomas Nelson Today

As we embrace the year 1998 and mark the two-hundreth anniversary of the Thomas Nelson company, we reflect on the fact that what began as a used bookstore on a side street of Edinburgh, Scotland, is today a NYSE company in America, leading the nation in the publication of Christian books, Bibles, and gift items.

A company that twenty-five years ago was essentially 80 percent reliant upon Bible sales is today a company that is 30 percent reliant on Bible sales, and yet we have doubled the Bible business in the last seven years. In 1976 we had $16 million in overall sales. Twenty-two years later we have grown closer to $250 million a year in sales.

Contributors to Success

How is it that we can report these figures? I think there are several answers to that question.

People Want to Know God

To me, one answer lies in the fact that, as they leave high school and college, today's young men and women have a longing to know God. There is an emptiness in the depth of their souls. They are searching for values, for relationships, for peace, and for salvation.

Our goal has been to be the company that will create the printed products to meet those needs. We don't market to one particular group such as the Baptists, the Methodists or the Presbyterians. We serve Christendom at large, worldwide. In one sense, nothing has changed since I bought the company back in 1969. I still want to produce books and Bibles that the vast majority of people across the spectrum of our society can read and understand.

There is an incarnational truth here. Just as two thousand years ago the eternal Son of God took upon Himself our human flesh and lived His life in the world, just as the inspired Word of God is brought to us via the properties of paper and ink, so a company like ours, which majors in bringing the unchanging gospel of Christ to the people, must do so out in the dog-eat-dog arena of business, cutthroat market competition, and taxes.

From the mid-1980s to the mid-1990s, Thomas Nelson experienced forty quarters that met or exceeded analysts' expectations. This is good news for a public company! In the last five of those years, we have taken the company from $75 million a year in sales to close to $250 million, an increase of more than 400 percent. We added overhead, we diversified the product line, and we changed the mix of the company.

The good news, at least in this world, doesn't always last forever. I mentioned our serious dip in 1995. Many of the retail stores went to what is called a "just-in-time" inventory. This means that the books we produced were stored on our warehouse shelves rather than on the bookstore's retail shelf, and only ordered and brought in to the store at the very last minute, just in time. So store owners no longer stocked the inventory as they always had in the past, they now wanted the publishers to assume that responsibility. This gave rise to a large number of just-in-time distributors.

Complicating that development is the fact that retail stores have grown from what used to be a mom-and-pop operations of three- to four-thousand square-foot buildings to the Barnes & Noble model of twenty-thousand square feet and over one hundred thousand titles in inventory. There are about two thousand of these super bookstores alone in 1998, which now occupy our giant malls and retail centers, some of them approaching twenty-five to thirty thousand square feet in area. Many retail bookstores having fifteen to twenty thousand titles have now virtually exploded into mega-stores with over one hundred thousand titles on their shelves.

As a result we now have a plethora of giant bookstores, far fewer family-owned stores, and not a whole lot more consumers. This meant for us a speed bump in product sales and a slowdown in turnover. As far as bookstores in general are concerned, I believe we are overbuilt today.

Having said that, even in this day of the Internet, I don't believe the monitor screen is ever going to replace the printed page. In fact, we at Thomas Nelson are using the technology of the Internet and the Web to make our products and catalogs available to the ever-growing techno-public.

Years ago people said that television would replace reading, but it never happened. There simply is no substitute for taking a book off the shelf and sitting up in bed, under a tree, on a porch, in front of the fireplace, or even in a little cave in the mountains of Lebanon, and reading it through with a relaxing cup of coffee. So we see the Internet as a creative way to increase our sales and for the marketing of books and Bibles that you can smell and touch and feel and, most importantly, read.

I Try to Be an Organized Entrepreneur

One of the great lessons I have had to learn over the years is to let go and delegate. To do it, you have got to be organized. If you have a growing business and you don't delegate, you perish. Dividing our business into units, or companies, has given me the game plan for delegation.

For example, our Bible unit has its own boss, Frank Couch. He is responsible for inventory, for sales, for the development of future products. Thus he is the general manager, or president, of that company. In the book business we have two companies, Word and Nelson. Now we have introduced a children's line called Tommy Nelson headed by Dan Johnson, and they develop children's books and audio. We have a specialty gift book division headed by Jack Countryman.

There are other units as well, and Ray Capp, our senior vice president, oversees a number of them. Joel Beasley runs the warehouse, Rusty Faulks heads up human resources. Mike Mitchell directs customer service, and Phil Derryberry handles information services. Other long-time personnel include Vance Lawson, vice president of finance; Phyllis Williams, our treasurer; Marion Shriner, controller; and Betty Ezell in our credit department.

Each of these units has its own budget. They report to proper management monthly the amount of sales, the amount of profit, and the amount of return on their assets. I review these results, looking through the numbers, meeting with the managers, keeping keenly aware of our progress.

Despite our size, today I still have less than eight people reporting to me. I try to meet with each of these managers at least once every week or two. I have endeavored to bring our gifted people up through the ranks of the company, so that more and more I am able to work myself out of a job.

We Emphasize Selling the Product

Just as in the beginning when our company specialized in selling door-to-door, to this day we place an incredibly strong emphasis on sales and marketing. We have one combined publishing sales force visiting virtually every major retail bookstore in America.

We've found that usually the buyer for the books and Bibles on the retail level is the same person. We have about fifty salespeople covering this arena. There are key accounts managers, too, and we have specialists calling on the general market as well.

However, in the gift division we have a sales force of over one hundred full-time people. The reason? There are about four times as many gift stores as there are bookstores—secular and religious.

Other crucial sales divisions for the company include international sales founded by Joe Ritchie and led today by Terry Draughon, ministry services headed up by Ted Squires, and Bill Sharp who heads up Nelson/Word Direct.

I believe the reason we are successful at Thomas Nelson is because we have our people out there showing the product and explaining its benefits.

I Employ the Win-Win Philosophy

I mentioned at the outset that Thomas Nelson historically was the first publishing company to employ a salesman to call on bookstores. This tradition of aggressive, low-pressure sales has continued right on through to the present.

To repeat, I am a great believer in delegating authority. All I ask is to be kept fully informed. We give our salespeople the opportunity to manage their own territories and, in that way, to be their own bosses. I do not hire a salesperson in whom I feel I cannot place my trust. So the Nelson sales force is made up of people who manage their own businesses. But our success goes far beyond good people with freedom to produce.

We enable our salespeople to own part of the company. A salesperson can set aside a small percentage of his total commission and the company will match it and put it in a special retirement plan. This means that every quarter, these people pick up a tidy sum of Thomas Nelson shares, which are set aside for future retirement. Several of our salespeople who stayed with the company over the years are worth over $1 million in their retirement program. Even today, a large percentage of the company is still owned by its employees.

For the key managers of our company, we also had an incentive plan as well. If a manager increased his or her profit by 12 percent over the previous year, he or she could put up to 10 percent of his or her salary and bonus aside for retirement and the company would match him or her with a 10 percent contribution. However, if the manager was clever enough to produce a 20 percent profit increase, the company would then match him or her on a two for one basis. Thus we had people who were setting aside a total of as much as 30 percent of their salary and bonus a year for retirement, becoming major owners in the company.

I call this my "win-win philosophy." The employees win, the shareholders win, and the company wins.

All along we have been very liberal with our people in terms of health insurance, hospitalization, life insurance, and other benefits, plus strong vacation incentives. Because of this, our company turnover has been very low, and even those who leave to launch out on their own into new opportunities regularly come back to say hello.

American by Choice

When I came to America to live in 1950, this was the most sought-after country in the world for young immigrants. Even today there are huge numbers of people in East Europe and the Third World who would give their right arms to be here. When you compare the standard of living in places like Eastern Europe, Russia, China, or India with what we have today, there is no contest. America remains the nation of plenty. We have about 6 percent of the world's population, and yet we possess more than 50 percent of the world's wealth. I still believe that the dream of almost every young person across the world is to be an American.

Gen. John Shalikashvili (Ret.), who succeeded Gen. Colin Powell as head of the Joint Chiefs of Staff, is a native of Poland.

His September 17, 1996, speech to newly naturalized citizens at the National Archives expressed his personal gratitude as an immigrant becoming a U.S. citizen. His remarks echo my own feelings, and so eloquently express my thoughts.

> I once heard someone ask, "What's the difference between the American Dream and everyone else's dream?" The answer is that "Everybody else's dream is to come to America." That's the dream, the dream to come to America, that binds us all together.

> For me, and for my parents, the dream came true in 1952, when we came to this magical place called America. A country where you know so well, if you work hard, you could become anything you wanted to be, a cowboy, a banker, a baker or even Chairman of the Joint Chiefs of Staff.

Note the general's encouraging words to the young men and women that day who might have thought the years for opportunity in America were gone.

> Today, as it was thirty-eight years ago, America is still a place with unlimited opportunities for those who work hard to realize their dreams we just talked about. Our success as a nation is based on the fact that although we come from so many different lands, we share a common set of beliefs about freedom, and about the dignity of man.

> For you, today, as it was for me in 1958, this is truly the dawn of a new day.

It doesn't matter how old or young you are, whether you're big or small, a man or a woman, for today you are Americans. Members of the greatest democracy in the history of man.

He closed his remarks by saying:

One of my officers told me of the day he attended the funeral of his grandmother, a few years ago. As he stood at the graveside, he said he was moved, not so much by the eulogy for his grandmother, but by what he saw on a nearby headstone.

For there, honoring a man with a distinctly East European name, his children, the man's children, had engraved the following words on his tombstone, "Thanks for bringing us to America, Dad."[1]

Despite the fact that over the last twenty-five years or so our government has had its hand in so much of our lives, making our people dependent upon bureaucracy and big handouts, there are still wonderful opportunities that exist here. Even though free enterprise and personal initiative seem to be continually under internal attack, I see some new signs of hope on the horizon. As I write, public pressure on Congress and the president to decrease government size and taxes to give people opportunity to be their own bosses is starting to work.

Looking back to my own upbringing, and as I look at America, I'm still acutely aware of how good we have it here. Truly God has blessed this nation. Consider our highway system and the air and rail services, highly dependable telephone, fax, and modem communications, and interstate trade. We have some of the most highly skilled workers in the world, and all of this in a free society to boot. To quote my mom, "We are by far still the *avant-garde* nation of the world."

However, there are places where we have slipped—like manufacturing. The reason is, of course, that you can get cheap labor in places like China, Mexico, and India. They can do a whole day's work there for less money than a person can earn in an hour's work here. As the world is shrinking because of growing levels of communication, we are going to have to face far more competition from across the globe. Think about it. When major news takes place in China, within minutes you're watching it on your television. The communication industry has transformed our world.

Another area in which we need to make far more progress is in overcoming what is still the problem of latent racial prejudice. My prayer to God is that we will find a way for blacks, whites, Hispanics, Asians, and others to work together for the good of one another and thus for the good of the nation. There are still some dark clouds of hatred hanging over our heads. I am an optimist, and I happen to believe God is still on the throne, and that through His grace we can find a way to work together to keep this nation great.

People and Productivity

Often I am asked why it is that immigrants so often excel in this country, far more so than even those who are born in America. I think there are a couple of answers.

First of all, anyone born anywhere tends to take his own country for granted. Most people who were born here with the wealth, the beauty, and sophisticated technology that surround them have never been exposed to the Third World, where there are continual poverty, hardship, and ill health.

There is another factor as well. Usually, the immigrant who comes here is very well educated, the cream of the crop. America admits the best of those who come from Asia, Europe, and the Middle East. They come here basically because they are gifted and they want to excel in what is still called the New World.

When you compare the best of this nation with the best of other nations, you will find that the best from other places have come here to work. They have a mind-set to compete and excel. So you are comparing a small group of immigrant people who are naturally gifted and committed to doing well versus our population at large here in America, who often have not been motivated in these same ways.

Remember the Pareto Principle which we discussed a few pages back: 20 percent of the people do 80 percent of the work and, conversely, 80 percent of the people do 20 percent of the work. In the bookstore business about 20 percent of our accounts produce 80 percent of our sales. Usually 20 percent of our publishing catalog produces 80 percent of the sales.

It makes me think back to the parable of the sower in the New Testament. Our Lord Jesus Christ taught us that of all the seed that was sown, only about 25 percent took root and grew and was fruitful. Jesus never gave us unrealistic expectations. He, who cared for the poor and, indeed, died and rose again for the world, also told us plainly, "For you have the poor with you always" (Matt. 26:11 NKJV).

Thus my view is that we are never called to clip the wings of the 20 percent who are producing the 80 percent. Let them keep producing!

One of the toughest things for me to do in business is to deal decisively with people or programs that continually underproduce. When you make a decision to cut your losses, often you are labeled ruthless. But honestly, it's that kind of hard-core decisiveness that makes the difference between success and failure. When you are under the authority of a board of directors and the shareholders, you're accountable. You have to be ready to limit your losses, and do so quickly. If you find there is no hope for positive change in a particular situation, if the ship keeps taking on water then the leak must be stopped!

On the other hand, if a person or a situation is salvageable, I will do everything in my power to try to support positive change. I will move people around, pay for schooling, or take whatever reasonable measures I can to try to find a way to bring a situation back to productivity. But if a person has simply lost the desire to be productive, there is little more that I or anyone else can do from that point on.

The killer for me is when I learn a person is dishonest. When the matter of sacred trust is lost, you have no choice but to close the book on the issue.

There is the human factor that all of us, even those in the top tiers of the 20 percent of productivity, will from time to time make mistakes. This is why most companies are ruled by boards, not just by individuals. King Solomon tipped us off to that reality thousands of years ago in the book of Proverbs: "In the multitude of counselors there is safety" (11:14 NKJV).

We who are in key positions in companies have got to select strong managers who can produce good results. But we can't look for perfection, and this is difficult for me. The issue is that the number of good decisions have got to outweigh the number of bad ones. If that happens, the balance sheet ends up on the plus side.

In publishing there are times you have to call off a book project. When you know you've got a loser, there is no reason to sit down and dillydally with it. Take your losses, find a new project, and let the loser go. When you do it, though, be prepared to take some grief from your critics in the 80 percentile. For me, when I see a cancer developing, I know it's too late for the medicine to work. It's time to schedule surgery.

Looking to the Future

People ask me, "Sam, what's going to happen to the company when you are off the scene?"

I have no doubt that it will continue to grow. I expect our role as a lighthouse for the people of God, and to the whole world, will be far greater in the next two hundred years than it has been in our first two centuries. We simply need to keep on growing in our ability to better communicate to the masses in our marketplace.

The company today has over 2,000 shareholders, a strong capital base, and over 1,200 employees who despise the word *quit*. In this year of our two-hundredth anniversary, we are breaking ground to more than double the size of our office headquarters and expand the warehouse. We are preparing for unprecedented growth in the years and decades ahead.

As we celebrate our first two hundred years, our personnel are centered in several different locations: Nashville, Dallas,

Atlanta, Miami, Connecticut, and Canada. Our goal is to congregate everyone together in fewer places. We are building and expanding across America, and this unified growth stands as a testimony to God's goodness and His blessing for the future.

Our company is gifted with incredible personnel. As we open the next two hundred years of our history, we have a matchless team of talented men and women in editorial, production, sales, and marketing who will give us the leadership we need for years to come. On the executive level, people in their thirties, forties, and fifties are being trained right now to run this business in the future and to carry the message of the gospel to future generations.

In the book of Hebrews, chapter 10, there is a characteristic trait that God possesses, and He seeks to pass it on to us. After promising us repeatedly in this passage, and in other places, that Jesus Christ died to forgive us all of our sins and trespasses, in verse 17 He makes a further point: "Their sins and their lawless deeds I will remember no more" (NKJV).

In other words, God both forgives and forgets.

As a Christian I find it is quite a bit easier to forgive than it is to forget. It's something I'm still working on. Honestly, I'd rather err on forgiving someone too much than not enough. I am a big believer in giving a sincere person a second chance, in large part because I have a God who has given me so many second chances.

This helps explains why by nature I am still after all these years an optimist.

Jesus said of the woman who wept at his feet, "Her sins . . . are forgiven, for she loved much. But to whom little is forgiven, the same loves little" (Luke 7:47 NKJV). The reason I tend to be a forgiving man is because I have been forgiven for so much myself. By God's grace, when we know we've been forgiven much, it becomes easier to pass His forgiveness on to other people.

Epilogue

Thanks

The apostle Paul said, "In everything give thanks; for this is the will of God in Christ Jesus for you" (1 Thess. 5:18 NKJV).

If I took that literally (which I do!) and gave thanks for everything here in these closing pages, it would triple the size of this book. So let me start with the personal, and move on to the corporate, the national, the world, and the other world.

Peggy, Joe, Sandra, and Rachel—thanks so much for giving me the opportunity to be your husband and dad. I don't need to tell you that at times I've been much better at being a law-giver than a peacemaker, a competitor than a consoler.

Peggy, it was God who brought you to me, and you are not only a beautiful lover of God, but a lover of me—honest, faithful, and persistent in staying by my side all these years. So many times I would travel the globe without notice, bring people home without warning, and, frankly, most women would not have put up with it. I bless God for your compassion, your hospitality, your love, and your warmth.

Joe, Sandra, and Rachel, you are an answer to your mother's and father's prayers. There were all those years we thought we would not have children, and here He has blessed us threefold—all three miracles, all three of you special.

Joe, you have brought us Julia, and the two of you have given us Ellery and Matthew Samuel. Sandra, you have brought Steve and Timothy to our family. Rachel, you're doing great in grad school with a wonderful life ahead of you.

I thank God daily for all three of you. Through the ups and downs of all our years together, you have brought me great joy and encouragement.

⋯⧉⋯

To my larger family at Thomas Nelson—my fellow employees, fellow shareholders, board of directors, trustees, all of you from the least to the greatest, the youngest to the oldest—what else can I say but, "You're the best!" I honestly never dreamed God would take us this far.

Each day we have the opportunity to bring again the Word of God to a parched and thirsty land. The Scriptures tell us to publish the glad tidings of peace (see Isa. 52:7) and we get to do that, over and over again. Though our days may be long and tiring, our mission together never gets old.

Thanks to all of you for a job so very well done.

I want to especially thank the board of directors currently serving all of us: Brownlee O. Currey Jr., W. Lipscomb Davis Jr., S. Joseph Moore, Robert J. Niebel Sr., Millard V. Oakley, Joe M. Rodgers, Cal Turner Jr., and Andrew Young. These are my bosses, the people who keep me on my toes. With a keen eye, they review company growth both financially and culturally. Friends and compatriots, I love you all! Let's keep getting it done together!

I want to give public thanks for the privilege of living in America. Where but in America could a shy and halting immigrant come and grow a company over a few short decades to what we have today, and to be secure as we look to the future? This sounds old-fashioned, but I am so grateful to be here that every time I see the flag flutter it gives me an indescribable feeling of warmth and gratitude. How proud I am to be in a land that adopted me and with open arms took me in.

Thanks, America, and please keep on being the land of the free and the home of the brave for the generations of people like me who are yet to arrive.

Finally, thank You, heavenly Father, together with Your Son and Holy Spirit, for offering me the opportunity to know You, to love You, and to serve You with all of my heart. Thank You for giving me the joy of Your salvation. Because of You, I look forward to eternity.

My prayer is that those who read this book will, like me and so many millions of others, turn themselves and their lives over to the Lord, inviting Him to enter and reign on the throne of their hearts, and that they will experience the comfort and joy of sins forgiven and a life that only Jesus Christ can give.

As a passerby, as a pilgrim here, and as one who brought nothing in and will take nothing out, my dream and my prayer for myself and for all of us is that we will each day commit ourselves and one another and all our lives unto Christ our God.